Fantastic and Getting Better!

Stories to remind us that GOD, Family, and Friends are what matter to make a Fantastic Day!

Vinton L. and M. Michele Stanfield

Tumbleweed Publishing

www.tumbleweedpublishing.com

www.libertyhousebandb.com

Liberty Hill, TX

We would like to acknowledge the following publishers and individuals for the following material. (Note: The stories that were taken from the public domain and where we could we listed who we thought were the authors.)

We would also like to thank the following family and friends that did the final review for us. Bob Rook, Victoria Panther, James and Astrid Tucker, Elizabeth Shaver.

Fantastic and Getting Better was compiled and authored by Vinton L. and M. Michele Stanfield, Tumbleweed Publishing.

All rights reserved. Printed in the United States of America. No part of this publication may be reproduced, stored in a retrieval system or transmitted in any form or by any means, electronic, mechanical, photocopying, recording or otherwise, without the written permission of the publisher.

ISBN 978-0-578-07363-7

Copyright @2010 by Tumbleweed Publishing

Publisher: Tumbleweed Publishing
             102 Independence Drive
             Liberty Hill, TX 78642-6234
             http://www.tumbleweedpublishing.com

Fantastic and Getting Better!

Introduction -

Vinton and Michele Stanfield consider themselves fortunate to have traveled 'throughout the world' for years. They have relished those opportunities that allowed them to live in many foreign countries, have taken pleasure in experiencing the different cultures, have learned a variety of languages, and continue to enjoy associations with their international friends.

After their first retirement, they lived on their 'blue-water' sailboat for more than ten years, traveling to many interesting ports. Love of family (especially their now 25 grandchildren and 2 great-grandchildren – *so far*) brought them back to Texas.

Vinton is retired military (Special Forces/Diplomatic Service), is a master woodworking craftsman, and a gourmet cook, having taken classes throughout the world.

Michele also served in the military (both Army and Air Force Air National Guard). She has worked overseas in Panama, Mexico, Bermuda, Turkey and Italy. Now she invests time in gardening, designing dried-flower cards, crafting and spending much of her time with the grandchildren.

They own and operate *Liberty House Bed and Breakfast* in Liberty Hill, Texas, *(www.libertyhousebandb.com)*, are volunteers for the American Red Cross and are Officers at their local Veterans of Foreign Wars Post.

Over the years they have received numerous emails from family and friends and some forwarded via unknown persons. Yet only a few have made their hearts skip a beat or say *"How true that is!"*

These short stories, poems and words of wisdom have conveyed feelings of love, warmth, and many a smile.

The original authors of these pieces are noted when possible. They have not been checked for authenticity, and in most parts of the book, they have been printed just the same as they were received.

We hope that you enjoy, as we have, reading these stories and that they will give you an insight as to how other people feel about GOD, Family and Friends.

It is our hope these stories will inspire you to say my day is

"Fantastic and Getting Better."

Vinton L. and M. Michele Stanfield

Table of Contents

A Different Christmas Poem 1
A Dog's Purpose 5
A Gallon of Milk 7
A Perfect Heart 11
A Soldier's Lullaby 13
Adam and Eve and Children 15
All Good Things 19
An Eye Opener 23
Are You There? 27
Bag of Nails 29
Bible in 50 Words 31
Checking In 33
Children Are... 37
Columbine High School 39
Communication…or Not! 43
Cowboy Poem 45
Dancing With God 49
Dear Dad 51
Dear God 53
DEATH 55
Deer Rop'in 57

Did Jesus Use a Modem?	63
Doesn't God Care Any More?	65
For You	69
Friends Are	71
Friends	75
Friendship	77
Funny Isn't It?	81
God in High School	83
God in the Grocery Store	85
God Knows Where I Am	87
God Said "NO"	91
God's Thoughts on Lawns	93
Great Truths	97
Guide to a Good Life	99
Have You Tasted My Jesus?	101
Having Mom Over for Dinner	103
Here in Your Heart	105
Hey, Wasn't That Us?	109
I Am Thankful…	113
I Dreamt That I Went to Heaven	115
I Found Jesus There	117
I Wish for You…	119
I Wished I Were You	121
Ice Cream for the Soul	123

If	125
If I Knew	127
I've Learned	129
John 3:16	133
Keeper	137
Kids	139
Lessons I Learned About Life	141
Life Under the Moonlight	143
Let's Run Through the Rain	145
Lord's Baseball Game	149
Meet ME in the Stair Well!	151
Remember Your ABC'S	153
Seems Almost Too Much To Handle	155
Senior Wedding	157
Seven Advices of Mevlâna	159
The Sack Lunch	161
The Wooden Bowl	165
Three Trees	169
To All the Kids Who Survived	173
T'was the Night Before Christmas	177
Unfolding the Rosebud	181
What Does Love Mean?	183
What God Can Do With Fifty-Seven Cents	187
What I Have Learned in Life!	189

What If…? 193
What Is Crucifixion? 195
What My Mother Taught Me 199
Why Didn't We Have a Drug Problem? 201
Why GOD Made Moms 203
Why Parents Have Grey Hair! 207
Woman and a Fork 209

A Different Christmas Poem

The embers glowed softly and in their dim light,
I gazed round the room and I cherished the sight.
My wife was asleep, her head on my chest,
My daughter beside me was angelic in rest.

Outside the snow fell, a blanket of white,
Transforming the yard to a winter delight.
The sparkling lights in the tree, I believe,
Completed the magic that was Christmas Eve.

My eyelids were heavy, my breathing was deep,
Secure and surrounded by love I would sleep.
In perfect contentment, or so it would seem,
So I slumbered, perhaps I started to dream.

The sound wasn't loud and it wasn't too near,
But I opened my eyes when it tickled my ear.
Perhaps just a cough, I didn't quite know,
Then the sure sound of footsteps outside in the snow.

My soul gave a tremble, I struggled to hear,
And I crept to the door just to see who was near.
Standing out in the cold and the dark of the night,
A lone figure stood, his face weary and tight.

A soldier, I puzzled, some twenty years old,
Perhaps a Marine, huddled here in the cold.
Alone in the dark, he looked up and smiled,
Standing watch over me, my wife and my child.

"What are you doing?" I asked without fear,
"Come in this moment, it's freezing out here!
Put down your pack, brush the snow from your sleeve,
You should be at home on a cold Christmas Eve!"

For barely a moment I saw his eyes shift,
Away from the cold and the snow blown in drifts.
To the window that danced with a warm fire's light,
Then he sighed and he said "It's really all right.
I'm out here by choice. I'm here every night."

"It's my duty to stand at the front of the line,
That separates you from the darkest of times.
No one had to ask or beg or implore me,
I'm proud to stand here like my fathers' before me."

"My Gramps died at 'Pearl' on a day in December,"
Then he sighed, "That's a Christmas Gram always remembers."
My Dad stood his watch in the jungles of 'Nam',
And now it is my turn and so, here I am."

"I've not seen my own son in more than a while,
But my wife sends me pictures; he's sure got her smile."
Then he bent and he carefully pulled from his bag,
The red, white, and blue...an American flag.

"I can live through the cold and the being alone,
Away from my family, my house and my home.
I can stand at my post through the rain and the sleet,
I can sleep in a foxhole with little to eat."

"I can carry the weight of killing another
Or lay down my life with my sisters and brothers.
Who stand at the front against any and all,
To ensure for all time that this flag will not fall."

"So go back inside," he said, "harbor no fright,
Your family is waiting and I'll be all right."
"But isn't there something I can do, at the least,

Give you money," I asked, "or prepare you a feast?
It seems all too little for all that you've done,
For being away from your wife and your son."

Then his eye welled a tear that held no regret,
"Just tell us you love us, and never forget
To fight for our rights back at home while we're gone;
To stand your own watch, no matter how long."

"For when we come home, either standing or dead,
To know you remember we fought and we bled.
Is payment enough, and with that we will trust,
That we mattered to you as you mattered to us."

The International War Veterans' Poetry Archive lists this poem as being written in December 2000 by Mr. Michael Marks, with the title "A Soldier's Christmas".

Vinton & Michele Stanfield

Airedale Mom and Pups

A Dog's Purpose

Being a veterinarian, I had been called to examine a ten-year-old Irish wolfhound named Belker. The dog's owners, Ron, his wife, Lisa, and their little boy, Shane, were all very attached to Belker, and they were hoping for a miracle.

I examined Belker and found he was dying of cancer. I told the family we couldn't do anything for Belker, and offered to perform the euthanasia procedure for the old dog in their home.

As we made arrangements, Ron and Lisa told me they thought it would be good for six-year-old Shane to observe the procedure. They felt as though Shane might learn something from the experience. The next day, I felt the familiar catch in my throat as Belker's family surrounded him. Shane seemed so calm, petting the old dog for the last time, that I wondered if he understood what was happening.

Within a few minutes, Belker slipped peacefully away. The little boy seemed to accept the dog's transition without any difficulty or confusion. We sat together for a while after Belker's death, wondering aloud about the sad fact that animal lives are shorter than human lives. Shane, who had been listening quietly, piped up, "I know why."

Startled, we all turned to him. What came out of his mouth next stunned me. I'd never heard a more comforting explanation. He said, "People are born so that they can learn how to live a good life -- like loving everybody all the time and being nice, right?" The six-year-old continued,

"Well, dogs already know how to do that, so they don't have to stay as long."

Dog's Rules…Enjoy every minute of every day!

Live simply. Love generously. Care deeply. Speak kindly.
Remember, if a dog was the teacher you would learn things like:
When loved ones come home, always run to greet them.
Never pass up the opportunity to go for a joyride.
Allow the experience of fresh air and the wind in your face to be pure ecstasy.
Take naps. Stretch before rising.
Run, romp, and play daily.
Thrive on attention and let people touch you.
Avoid biting when a simple growl will do.
On warm days, stop to lie on your back on the grass.
On hot days, drink lots of water and lie under a shady tree.
When you're happy, dance around and wag your entire body.
Eat with gusto and enthusiasm.
Stop when you have had enough.
Be loyal. Never pretend to be something you're not.
If what you want lies buried, dig until you find it.
When someone is having a bad day, be silent, sit close by and nuzzle them gently.
Always be grateful for each new day and for the blessing of you.

A Gallon of Milk

A young man had been to Wednesday night Bible Study. The Pastor had shared ideas about listening to God and obeying the Lord's voice. The young man couldn't help but wonder, *"Does God still speak to people?"* After service he went out with some friends for coffee and pie and they discussed the message.

Several different ones talked about how God had led them in different ways. It was about ten o'clock when the young man started driving home. Sitting in his car, he just began to pray, "God...if You still speak to people, speak to me. I will listen. I will do my best to obey."

As he drove down the main street of his town, he had the strangest thought to stop and buy a gallon of milk. He shook his head and said out loud, "God, is that you?" He didn't get a reply and started toward home but again, the thought, *buy a gallon of milk.*

The young man thought about Samuel and how he didn't recognize the voice of God, and how little Samuel ran to Eli.

"Okay, God, in case that is you, I will buy the milk." It didn't seem like too hard a test of obedience. He could always use the milk. He stopped and purchased the gallon of milk and started off toward home.

As he passed Seventh Street, he again felt the urge, *Turn down that street.* *This is crazy* he thought and drove on past the intersection. Again, he felt that he should turn down Seventh Street. At the next intersection, he turned back and headed down Seventh. Half jokingly, he said out loud, "Okay, God, I will."

He drove several blocks, when suddenly, he felt like he should stop. He pulled over to the curb and looked around. He was in a semi-commercial area of town. It wasn't the best but it wasn't the worst of neighborhoods either. The businesses were closed and most of the houses looked dark like the people were already in bed.

Again, he sensed something, *Go and give the milk to the people in the house across the street.* The young man looked at the house. It was dark and it looked like the people were either gone or they were already asleep. He started to open the door and then sat back in the car seat.

"Lord, this is insane. Those people are asleep and if I wake them up, they are going to be mad and I will look stupid." Again, he felt like he should go and give the milk.

Finally, he opened the door, "Okay God, if this is You, I will go to the door and I will give them the milk. If You want me to look like a crazy person, okay. I want to be obedient. I guess that will count for something but if they don't answer right away, I am out of here." He walked across the street and rang the bell. He could hear some noise inside. A man's voice yelled out, "Who is it? What do you want?" Then the door opened before the young man could get away. The other man was standing there in his jeans and T-shirt. He looked like he just got out of bed. He had a strange look on his face and he didn't seem too happy to have some stranger standing on his doorstep. "What is it?" The young man thrust out the gallon of milk, "Here, I brought this to you." The man took the milk and rushed down a hallway.

Then from down the hall came a woman carrying the milk toward the kitchen. The man was following her holding a baby. The baby was crying. The man had tears streaming down his face. The man began speaking and half crying, "We were just praying. We had some big bills this month and we ran out of money. We didn't have any milk for our baby. I was just praying and asking God to show me how to get some milk."

His wife in the kitchen yelled out, "I asked him to send an angel with some milk. Are you an angel?"

The young man reached into his wallet and pulled out all the money he had on him and put in the man's hand. He turned and walked back toward his car and the tears were streaming down his face.

He knew that God still answers prayers.

Five Generations

A Perfect Heart

One day a young man was standing in the middle of the town proclaiming that he had the most beautiful heart in the whole valley. A large crowd gathered and they all admired his heart for it was perfect. There was not a mark or a flaw in it. Yes, they all agreed it truly was the most beautiful heart they had ever seen. The young man was very proud and boasted more loudly about his beautiful heart.

Suddenly, an old man appeared at the front of the crowd and said, "Why, your heart is not nearly as beautiful as mine." The crowd and the young man looked at the old man's heart. It was beating strongly but full of scars. It had places where pieces had been removed and other pieces added. They didn't fit quite right and there were several jagged edges. In fact, in some places there were deep gouges where whole pieces were missing. The people stared and thought, *how can he say his heart is more beautiful?*

The young man looked at the old man's heart and saw its state and laughed. "You must be joking," he said. "Compare your heart with mine, mine is perfect and yours is a mess of scars and tears." "Yes," said the old man, "Yours is perfect looking, but I would never trade with you. You see, every scar represents a person to whom I have given my love. I tear out a piece of my heart and give it to them, and often they give me a piece of their heart, which fits into an empty place in my heart. The pieces aren't exact. I have some rough edges, which I cherish, because they remind me of the love we shared. Sometimes I have given pieces of my heart away, and the other person hasn't returned a piece of his heart to me. These are the empty gouges. Giving love is taking a chance. Although these gouges are painful, they stay open, reminding me of the love I have for these people too, and I hope someday they may return and fill the space I have waiting. So now do you see what true beauty is?"

The young man stood silently with tears running down his cheeks. He walked up to the old man, reached into his perfect young and beautiful heart, and ripped out a piece. He offered it to the old man with trembling hands. The old man took his offering, placed it in his heart and then took a piece from his old scarred heart and placed it in the wound in the young man's heart. It fit, but not perfectly, as there were some jagged edges. The young man looked at his heart, not perfect anymore but more beautiful than ever, since love from the old man's heart flowed into his. They embraced and walked away side by side. How sad it must be to go through life with a whole heart.

A Soldier's Lullaby
(Taps)

"*Taps*" is a famous musical piece, sounded by the U.S. military nightly to indicate that it is 'lights out' and also during flag ceremonies and funerals, generally on bugle or trumpet. The tune is also sometimes known as "Butterfield's Lullaby" or by the lyrics of its second verse, "Day is Done".

The tune is actually a variation of an earlier bugle call known as the "Scott Tattoo" which was used in the U.S. from 1835 until 1860. It was arranged in its present form by the Union Army Brigadier General Daniel Butterfield. He was an American Civil War general who commanded the 3rd Brigade of the 1st Division in the V Army Corps of the Army of the Potomac while at Harrison's Landing, Virginia in July 1862. To replace a previous French bugle call used to signal 'lights out', Butterfield's bugler, Oliver W. Norton, of Erie, Pennsylvania, was the first to sound the new call. Within months, *Taps* was used by both Union and Confederate forces.

Taps concludes many military funerals conducted with honors at Arlington National Cemetery, as well as hundreds of others around the United States. The tune is also sounded at many memorial services in Arlington's Memorial Amphitheater and at gravesites throughout the cemetery.

Taps is sounded during each of the 2,500 military wreath ceremonies conducted at the Tomb of the Unknowns every year, including the ones held on Memorial Day. The ceremonies are viewed by many people, including veterans, school groups, and foreign officials. *Taps* is also sounded nightly in military installations at non-deployed locations to indicate that it is 'lights out'. When *Taps* is sounded at a funeral, it is customary for serving members of the military or veterans to salute. The corresponding gesture for civilians is to place the right hand over the heart.

TAPS

Day is done, gone the sun
From the lakes, from the hills, from the sky
All is well, safely rest
God is near.

Fading light dims the sight
And a star gems the sky, gleaming bright
From afar, drawing near
Falls the night.

Thanks and praise for our days
Neath the sun, neath the stars, neath the sky
As we go, this we know
God is near.

Adam and Eve and Children

After creating heaven and earth, God created Adam and Eve. The first thing he said to them was "DON'T!"

"Don't what?" Adam replied.

"Don't eat the forbidden fruit." God said.

"Forbidden fruit? We have forbidden fruit? Hey Eve...we have forbidden fruit!!!!!"

"No way!"

"Yes way!"

"Do NOT eat the fruit!" said God.

"Why?"

"Because I am your Father and I said so!" God replied, wondering why He hadn't stopped creation after making the elephants. A few minutes later, God saw His children having an apple break and He was ticked!

"Didn't I tell you not to eat the fruit?" God asked.

"Uh huh," Adam replied.

"Then why did you?" said the Father.

"I don't know," said Eve.

"She started it!" Adam said

"Did not!"

"Did to!"

"DID NOT!"

Having had it with the two of them, God's punishment was that Adam and Eve should have children of their own. Thus the pattern was set and it has never changed.

BUT THERE IS REASSURANCE IN THE STORY!

If you have persistently and lovingly tried to give children wisdom and they haven't taken it, don't be hard on yourself. If God had trouble raising children, what makes you think it would be a piece of cake for you?

THINGS TO THINK ABOUT:

1. You spend the first two years of their life teaching them to walk and talk. Then you spend the next sixteen telling them to sit down and shut up.
2. Grandchildren are God's reward for not killing your own children.
3. Mothers of teens now know why some animals eat their young.
4. Children seldom misquote you. In fact, they usually repeat word for word what you shouldn't have said.
5. The main purpose of holding children's parties is to remind yourself that there are children more awful than your own.
6. We child-proofed our homes but they are still getting inside.

ADVICE FOR THE DAY!

Be nice to your kids. They will choose your nursing home.

AND FINALLY: IF YOU HAVE A LOT OF TENSION AND YOU GET A HEADACHE, DO WHAT IT SAYS ON THE ASPIRIN BOTTLE: "TAKE TWO ASPIRIN" AND "KEEP AWAY FROM CHILDREN."

Vinton & Michele Stanfield

"Don't think I did it!"

All Good Things

He was in the first through third grade classes I taught at Saint Mary's School in Morris, Minnesota. All 34 of my students were dear to me but Mark Eklund was one in a million. He was very neat in appearance but had that happy-to-be-alive attitude that made even his occasional mischievousness delightful.

Mark talked incessantly. I had to remind him again and again that talking without permission was not acceptable. What impressed me so much, though, was his sincere response every time I had to correct him for misbehaving – "Thank you for correcting me, Sister!" I didn't know what to make of it at first but before long I became accustomed to hearing it many times a day.

One morning my patience was growing thin when Mark talked once too often and then I made a novice-teacher's mistake. I looked at Mark and said, "If you say one more word, I am going to tape your mouth shut!" It wasn't ten seconds later when Chuck blurted out, "Mark is talking again." I hadn't asked any of the students to help me watch Mark, but since I had stated the punishment in front of the class, I had to act on it. I remember the scene as if it had occurred this morning. I walked to my desk, very deliberately opened my drawer and took out a roll of masking tape. Without saying a word, I proceeded to Mark's desk, tore off two pieces of tape and made a big X with them over his mouth. I then returned to the front of the room. As I glanced at Mark to see how he was doing, he winked at me. That did it! I started laughing. The class cheered as I walked back to Mark's desk, removed the tape, and shrugged my shoulders. His first words were, "Thank you for correcting me, Sister."

At the end of the year, I was asked to teach junior-high math. The years flew by and before I knew it Mark was in my classroom again. He was more handsome than ever and just as polite. Since he had to listen carefully to my instruction in the 'new math', he did not talk as much in the ninth grade as he had in the third. One Friday, things just didn't feel right. We had worked hard on a new concept all week and I sensed that the students were frowning, frustrated with themselves and edgy with one another. I had to stop this crankiness before it got out of hand. So, I asked them to list the names of the other students in the room on two sheets of paper, leaving a space between each name. Then I told them to think of the nicest thing they could say about each of their classmates and write it down. It took the remainder of the class period to finish their assignment and as the students left the room, each one handed me the papers. Mark said, "Thank you for teaching me, Sister. Have a good weekend."

That Saturday, I wrote down the name of each student on a separate sheet of paper and I listed what everyone else had said about that individual. On Monday, I gave each student his or her list. Before long, the entire class was smiling. "Really?" I heard whispered. "I never knew that meant anything to anyone!" "I didn't know others liked me so much." No one ever mentioned those papers in class again. I never knew if they discussed them after class or with their parents but it didn't matter. The exercise had accomplished its purpose. The students were happy with themselves and one another again.

That group of students moved on as did others. Several years later, after I returned from vacation, my parents met me at the airport. As we were driving home, Mother asked me the usual questions about the trip, the weather, and my experiences in general. There was a lull in the conversation. Mother gave Dad a side-ways glance and I simply said, "Dad?" My father cleared his throat as he usually did before something important. "The Eklunds called last night," he began. "Really?" I said. "I haven't heard from them in years. I wonder how Mark is." Dad responded quietly. "Mark was killed in Vietnam," he said. "The funeral is tomorrow, and his parents would like it if you could attend." To this day I can still point to the exact spot driving on I-494 where Dad told me about Mark. I had never before seen a serviceman in a military coffin. Mark looked so handsome, so mature. All I could think at that moment was, *'Mark I would give all the masking tape in the world if only you would talk to me.'*

The church was packed with Mark's friends. Chuck's sister sang "The Battle Hymn of the Republic." Why did it have to rain on the day of the funeral? It was difficult enough at the graveside. The pastor said the usual prayers and the bugler played "Taps". One by one, those who loved Mark took a last walk by the coffin and sprinkled it with holy water. I was the last one to bless the coffin. As I stood there, one of the soldiers who acted as pallbearer came up to me. "Were you Mark's math teacher?" he asked. I nodded as I continued to stare at the coffin. "Mark talked about you a lot," he said.

After the funeral, most of Mark's former classmates headed to Chuck's farmhouse for lunch. Mark's mother and father were there, obviously waiting for me. "We want to show you something," his father said, taking a wallet out of his pocket. "They found this on Mark when he was killed. We thought you might recognize it." Opening the billfold, he carefully removed two worn pieces of notebook paper that had obviously been taped, folded and refolded many times. I knew without looking that the papers were the ones on which I had listed all the good things each of Mark's classmates had said about him. "Thank you so much for doing that," Mark's mother said. "As you can see, he treasured it." Mark's classmates started to gather around us. Charlie smiled rather sheepishly and said, "I still have my list. It's in the top drawer of my desk at home." Chuck's wife said, "Chuck asked me to put his in our wedding album." "I have mine too," Marilyn said. "It's in my diary." Then Vicki, another classmate, reached into her pocketbook, took out her wallet and showed her worn and frazzled list to the group. "I carry this with me at all times," Vicki said without batting an eyelash. "I think we all saved our lists." That's when I finally sat down and cried. I cried for Mark and for all his friends, who would never see him again.

Written by: Sister Helen P. Mrosla

An Eye Opener

THIS STORY IS TRULY AN EYE OPENER. This story was written by a doctor who worked in South Africa.

One night I had worked hard to help a mother in the labor ward; but in spite of all we could do she died, leaving us with a tiny premature baby and a crying two-year-old daughter. We would have difficulty keeping the baby alive, as we had no incubator. (We had no electricity to run an incubator.) We also had no special feeding facilities. Although we lived on the equator, nights were often chilly with treacherous drafts.

One student midwife went for the box we had for such babies and the cotton wool in which the baby would be wrapped. Another went to stoke up the fire and fill a hot water bottle. She came back shortly in distress to tell me that in filling the bottle, it had burst. Rubber perishes easily in tropical climates. "And it is our last hot water bottle!" she exclaimed. As in the West it is no good crying over spilled milk, so in Central Africa it might be considered no good crying over burst water bottles. They do not grow on trees and there are no drugstores down jungle pathways.

"All right," I said, "put the baby as near the fire as you safely can and sleep between the baby and the door to keep it free from drafts. Your job is to keep the baby warm."

The following noon, as I did most days, I went to have prayers with many of the orphanage children who chose to gather with me. I gave the youngsters various suggestions of things about which to pray and told them about the tiny baby. I explained our problem about keeping the baby warm enough, mentioning the hot water bottle. The baby could so easily die if it got chills. I also told them of the two-year-old sister, crying because her mother had died.

During the prayer time, one ten-year-old girl, Ruth, prayed with the usual blunt conciseness of our African children. "Please, God," she prayed, "Send us a water bottle. It'll be no good tomorrow, God, as the baby will be dead, so please send it this afternoon."

While I gasped inwardly at the audacity of the prayer, she added by way of a corollary, "And while You are about it, would You please send a dolly for the little girl so she'll know You really love her?"

As often with children's prayers, I was put on the spot. Could I honestly say, "Amen?" I just did not believe that God could do this. Oh, yes, I know that He can do everything. The Bible says so but there are limits, aren't there? The only way God could answer this particular prayer would be by sending me a parcel from the homeland. I had been in Africa for almost four years at that time, and I had never, ever received a parcel from home. Anyway, if anyone did send me a parcel, who would put in a hot water bottle? I lived on the equator!

Halfway through the afternoon, while I was teaching in the nurses' training school, a message was sent that there was a car at my front door. By the time I reached home, the car had gone, but there, on the veranda, was a large twenty-two pound parcel. I felt tears pricking my eyes. I could not open the parcel alone, so I sent for the orphanage children. Together we pulled off the string, carefully undoing each knot. We folded the paper, taking care not to tear it unduly. Excitement was mounting.

Some thirty or forty pairs of eyes were focused on the large cardboard box. From the top, I lifted out brightly colored, knitted jerseys. Eyes sparkled as I gave them to the children. There were the knitted bandages for the leprosy patients and the children looked a little bored.

Then came a box of mixed raisins and other food items. As I put my hand in again, I felt the...could it really be? I grasped it and pulled it out – "Yes, a brand-new, rubber hot water bottle," I cried.

I had not asked God to send it. I had not truly believed that He could. Ruth was in the front row of the children. She rushed forward, crying out, "If God has sent the bottle, then He must have sent the dolly, too!"

Rummaging down to the bottom of the box, she pulled out the small, beautifully dressed dolly. Her eyes shone! She had never doubted! Looking up at me, she asked, "Can I go over with you, Mummy, and give this dolly to that little girl, so she'll know that Jesus really loves her?"

That parcel had been on the way for five whole months. Packed up by my former Sunday school class, whose leader had heard and obeyed God's prompting to send a hot water bottle, even to the equator. One of the girls had put in a dolly for an African child -- five months before -- in answer to the believing prayer of a ten-year-old to bring it 'that afternoon'.

"Before they call, I will answer!" Isaiah 65:24

Are You There?

A little boy, who was 'very' much afraid of the dark, was told by his mother to go out to the back porch and bring her the broom.

The little boy turned to his mother and said, "Mama, I don't want to go out there. It's dark." The mother smiled reassuringly at her son. "You don't have to be afraid of the dark," she explained, "Jesus is out there. He'll look after you and protect you."

The little boy looked at his mother real hard and asked, "Are you sure He's out there?"

"Yes, I'm sure. He is everywhere and is always ready to help you when you need Him." she said.

The little boy thought about that for a minute and then went to the back door and cracked it a little. Peering out into the darkness, he called, "Jesus? If you're out there, would you please hand me the broom?"

Vinton & Michele Stanfield

"You want me to do what?"

Bag of Nails

There once was a little boy who had a bad temper. His father gave him a bag of nails and told him that every time he lost his temper, he must hammer a nail into the back of the fence.

The first day the boy had driven 37 nails into the fence. Over the next few weeks, as he learned to control his anger, the number of nails hammered daily gradually dwindled. He discovered it was easier to hold his temper than to drive those nails into the fence. Finally, the day came when the boy didn't lose his temper at all.

He told his father about this and the father suggested that the boy now pull out one nail for each day that he was able to hold his temper. The days passed and the young boy was able to tell his father that all the nails were gone.

The father took his son by the hand and led him to the fence. He said, "You have done well, my son, but look at the holes in the fence. The fence will never be the same. When you say things in anger, they leave a scar just like this one. You can put a knife in a man and draw it out. It won't matter how many times you say I'm sorry, the wound is still there. A verbal wound is as bad as a physical one. Friends are very rare jewels, indeed. They make you smile and encourage you to succeed. They lend an ear, they share words of praise and they always want to open their hearts to us.

"...Everyone should be quick to listen, slow to speak and slow to become angry..." James 1:19

Bible in 50 Words

*God made
*Adam bit
*Noah arked
*Abraham split
*Joseph ruled
*Jacob fooled
*Bush talked
*Moses balked
*Pharaoh plagued
*People walked
*Sea divided
*Tablets guided
*Promise landed
*Saul freaked
*David peeked
*Prophets warned
*Jesus born
*God walked
*Love talked
*Anger crucified
*Hope died
*Love rose
*Spirit flamed
*Word spread
*God remained...

"Why do I have to do all the cooking?"

Checking In

A minister, passing through his church in the middle of the day, decided to pause by the altar and see who had come to pray.

Just then the back door opened and a man came down the aisle. The minister frowned as he saw that the man hadn't shaved in a while. His shirt was kind of shabby and his coat was worn and frayed. The man knelt; he bowed his head, then rose and walked away.

In the days that followed each noon time came this chap, each time he knelt just for a moment, a lunch pail in his lap.

Well, the minister's suspicions grew. With robbery a main fear, he stopped the man and asked him, "What are you doing here?" The old man said he worked down the road and lunch was half an hour. Lunchtime was his prayer time, for finding strength and power.

"I stay only moments, see, because the factory is so far away; as I kneel here talking to the Lord, this is what I say:

I JUST CAME AGAIN TO TELL YOU, LORD, HOW HAPPY I'VE BEEN, SINCE WE FOUND EACH OTHER'S FRIENDSHIP AND YOU TOOK AWAY MY SIN. DON'T KNOW MUCH OF HOW TO PRAY, BUT I THINK ABOUT YOU EVERYDAY. SO, JESUS, THIS IS JIM CHECKING IN TODAY."

The minister, feeling foolish, told Jim that he was welcome to come and pray just anytime.

"Time to go," Jim smiled, and said "Thanks." He hurried to the door. The minister knelt at the altar. His cold heart melted, warmed with love, and met with Jesus there. As the tears flowed, in his heart as he repeated old Jim's prayer:

"I JUST CAME AGAIN TO TELL YOU, LORD, HOW HAPPY I'VE BEEN, SINCE WE FOUND EACH OTHER'S FRIENDSHIP AND YOU TOOK AWAY MY SIN. I DON'T KNOW MUCH OF HOW TO PRAY, BUT I THINK ABOUT YOU EVERYDAY. SO, JESUS, THIS IS ME CHECKING IN TODAY."

Past noon, one day, the minister noticed that old Jim hadn't come. As more days passed without Jim he began to worry some. At the factory, he asked about him, learning he was ill. The hospital staff was worried, but he'd given them a thrill.

The week that Jim was with them brought changes in the ward. His smiles, a contagious joy, changed people, were his reward. The head nurse couldn't understand why Jim was so glad, when no flowers, calls or cards came, not a visitor.

As the minister stayed by his bed, he voiced the nurse's concern. No friends came to show they cared. He had nowhere to turn. Looking surprised, old Jim spoke up and with a winsome smile; "the nurse is wrong, she couldn't know, that in here all the while; everyday at noon He's here, a dear friend of mine, you see, He sits right down, takes my hand, leans over and says to me:

I JUST CAME AGAIN TO TELL YOU, JIM, HOW HAPPY I HAVE BEEN, SINCE WE FOUND THIS FRIENDSHIP, AND I TOOK AWAY YOUR SIN. ALWAYS LOVE TO HEAR YOU PRAY, I THINK ABOUT YOU EACH DAY, AND SO JIM, THIS IS JESUS CHECKING IN TODAY."

Vinton & Michele Stanfield

Truck Load of Trouble

Children Are...

Amazing, acknowledge them.
Believable, trust them.
Childlike, allow them.
Divine, honor them.
Energetic, nourish them.
Fallible, embrace them.
Gifts, treasure them.
Here Now, be with them.
Innocent, delight with them.
Joyful, appreciate them.
Kind-hearted, learn from them.
Lovable, cherish them.
Magical, fly with them.
Noble, esteem them.
Open-minded, respect them.
Precious, value them.
Questioners, encourage them.
Resourceful, support them.
Spontaneous, enjoy them.
Talented, believe in them.
Unique, affirm them.
Vulnerable, protect them.

Whole, recognize them.

Xtra-special, celebrate them.

Yearning, notice them.

Zany, laugh with them.

Grandparents and grandchildren,
Together, they create a chain of love
Linking the past,
With the future.
The chain may lengthen,
But it will never part.

Our Grandchildren fill our hearts with pleasure,
Each a joy for us to treasure.
For in this world of stress and strife,
Each is the reward for a good, long life.

Columbine High School

Please read this painfully truthful speech given by Rachel Scott's father before the US Judiciary Committee.

On Thursday, May 27, 1999, Darrell Scott, the father of Rachel Scott, a victim of the Columbine High School shootings in Littleton, Colorado, was invited to speak to the House Judiciary Committee's Sub-committee. What he said to them was painfully truthful. They were not prepared to hear what he was to say, nor was it received well. It needed to be heard by every parent, teacher, politician, sociologist, psychologist and every so-called expert. These courageous words spoken by Darrell Scott are powerful, penetrating and deeply personal. There is no doubt that he felt a need to express himself as a voice crying in the wilderness. Following is a portion of the transcript:

"Since the dawn of creation, there has been good and evil in the hearts of men and women. We all contain seeds of kindness or seeds of violence. The death of my wonderful daughter, Rachel Joy Scott, and the deaths of that heroic teacher and the eleven other children must not be in vain. Their blood cries out for answers.

The first recorded act of violence was when Cain slew his brother, Abel, out in the field. The villain was not the club he used neither was it the National *Club* Association. The true killer was Cain, and the real reason for the murder could only be found in Cain's heart. In the days that followed the Columbine tragedy, I was amazed at how quickly fingers began to be pointed at groups such as the NRA.

I am not a member of the NRA. I am not a hunter. I do not even own a gun. I am not here to defend or represent the NRA because I do not believe that they are responsible for my daughter's death. Therefore, I do not believe that they need to be defended. If I believed that they had anything to do with Rachel's murder, I would be their strongest opponent.

I am here, today, to declare that Columbine was not just a tragedy. It was a spiritual event that should be forcing us to look at where the real blame lies. Much of the blame lies here in this room, behind the pointing fingers of the accusers themselves.

I wrote a poem just four nights ago that best expresses my feelings. This was written way before I knew I would be speaking here today.

> Your laws ignore our deepest needs,
> Your words are empty air.
> You've stripped away our heritage,
> You've outlawed simple prayer.
> Now gunshots fill our classrooms,
> And precious children die.
> You seek for answers everywhere,
> And ask the question, "Why?"
> You regulate restrictive laws

> Through legislative creed.
> And yet you fail to understand
> That God is what we need.

Men and women are three-part beings. We all consist of body, soul and spirit. When we refuse to acknowledge a third part of our make-up, we create a void that allows evil, prejudice and hatred to rush in and create havoc. Spiritual influences were present within our educational systems for most of our nation's history. Many of our major colleges began as theological seminaries. This is a historical fact. What has happened to us as a nation? We have refused to honor God and in so doing we open the doors to hatred and violence. Then, when something, as terrible as Columbine's tragedy occurs, politicians immediately seek to pass more restrictive laws that contribute to erode away our personal and private liberties. We do not need more restrictive laws.

Eric and Dylan would not have been stopped by metal detectors. No amount of gun laws can stop someone who spends months planning this type of massacre. The real villain lies within our own hearts.

Political posturing and restrictive legislation are not the answers. The young people of our nation hold the key. There is a spiritual awakening taking place that will not be squelched! We do not need more religion, or more gaudy television evangelists spewing out verbal religious garbage.

We do not need more million-dollar church buildings built while people with basic needs are being ignored. We do need a change of heart and a humble acknowledgment that this nation was founded on the principle of simple trust in God.

As my son Craig lay under that table in the school library and saw his two friends murdered before his very eyes, he did not hesitate to pray in school. I defy any law or politician to deny him that right. I challenge every young person in America, and around the world, to realize that on April 20, 1999 at Columbine High School prayer was brought back into our schools."

Communication...or Not!

A judge was interviewing a woman regarding her pending divorce, and asked, "What are the grounds for your divorce?"

She replied, "About four acres and a nice little home in the middle of the property with a stream running nearby."

"No," he said, "I mean what is the foundation of this case?"

"It is made of concrete, brick and mortar," she responded.

"I mean," he continued, "What are your relations like?"

"I have an aunt and uncle living here in town and so do my husband's parents."

He said, "Do you have a real grudge?"

"No," she replied, "We have a two-car carport and have never really needed one."

"Please," he tried again, "is there any infidelity in your marriage?"

"Yes, both my son and daughter have stereo sets. We don't necessarily like the music but the answer to your questions is yes."

"Ma'am, does your husband ever beat you up?"

"Yes," she responded, "about twice a week he gets up earlier than I do."

Finally, in frustration, the judge asked, "Lady, why do you want a divorce?"

"Oh, I don't want a divorce," she replied. "I've never wanted a divorce. My husband does. He said he can't communicate with me!"

Communication...or Not!

A judge was interviewing a woman regarding her pending divorce, and asked, "What are the grounds for your divorce?"

She replied, "About four acres and a nice little home in the middle of the property with a stream running nearby."

"No," he said, "I mean what is the foundation of this case?"

"It is made of concrete, brick and mortar," she responded.

"I mean," he continued, "What are your relations like?"

"I have an aunt and uncle living here in town and so do my husband's parents."

He said, "Do you have a real grudge?"

"No," she replied, "We have a two-car carport and have never really needed one."

"Please," he tried again, "is there any infidelity in your marriage?"

"Yes, both my son and daughter have stereo sets. We don't necessarily like the music but the answer to your questions is yes."

"Ma'am, does your husband ever beat you up?"

"Yes," she responded, "about twice a week he gets up earlier than I do."

Finally, in frustration, the judge asked, "Lady, why do you want a divorce?"

"Oh, I don't want a divorce," she replied. "I've never wanted a divorce. My husband does. He said he can't communicate with me!"

Cowboy Poem

I ain't much for shopping,
Or for goin' into town.
Except at cattle-shipping time,
 I ain't too easily found.

But the day came when
I had to go - I left the kids with Ma.
But 'fore I left, she asked me,
"Would you pick me up a bra?"

So without thinkin' I said, "Sure."
How tough could that job be?
An' I bent down and kissed her,
An' said, "I'll be back by three."

Well, I done the things I needed,
But I started to regret.
Ever offering to buy that thing
It worked me up a sweat.

I walked into the ladies shop
My hat pulled over my eyes.
I didn't want to take a chance
On bein' recognized.

I walked up to the sales clerk,
I didn't hem or haw.
I told that lady right straight out,
"I'm here to buy a bra."

From behind I heard some snickers,
So, I turned around to see
Every woman in that store
Was a'gawkin' right at me!

"What kind would you be looking for?"
Well, I just scratched my head.
I'd only seen one kind before,
"Thought bras was bras," I said.

She gave me a disgusted look,
"Well sir, that's where you're wrong.
Follow me," I heard her say,
Like a dog, I tagged along.

She took me down this aisle
Where bras were on display.
I thought my jaw would hit the floor
When I saw that lingerie.

They had all these different styles
That I'd never seen before.
I thought I'd go plumb crazy
'fore I left that women's store.

They had bras you wear for eighteen hours
And bras that cross your heart.
There were bras that lift and separate,
And that was just the start.

They had bras that made you feel
Like you ain't wearing one at all,
And bras that you can train in
When you start off when you're small.

Well, I finally made my mind up.
Picked a black and lacy one.
I told the lady, "Bag it up."
And figured I was done.

But then she asked me for the size,
I didn't hesitate.
I knew that measurement by heart,
"A six and seven-eighths."

"Six and seven-eighths, you say?
 That really isn't right."
"Oh, yes ma'am! I'm real positive.
I measured them last night!"

I thought that she'd go into shock.
Musta' took her by surprise,
When I told her that my wife's bust
Was the same as my hat size.

"That's what I used to measure with,
I figured it was fair.
But if I'm wrong, I'm sorry ma'am."
This drew another stare.

By now a crowd had gathered
And they all was crackin' up.
When the lady asked to see my hat
To measure for the cup.

When she finally had it figured,
I gave the gal her pay.
Then I turned to leave the store,
Tipped my hat and said, "Good day."

My wife had heard the story
'fore I ever made it home.
She'd talked to fifteen women
Who called her on the phone.

She was still a laughin'
But by then I didn't care.
Now she don't ask and I don't shop
For women's underwear.

Dancing With God

When I meditated on the word Guidance, I kept seeing 'dance' at the end of the word. I remember reading that doing God's will is a lot like dancing.

When two people try to lead, nothing feels right. The movement doesn't flow with the music and everything is quite uncomfortable and jerky. When one person realizes that and lets the other lead, both bodies begin to flow with the music. One gives gentle cues, perhaps with a nudge to the back or by pressing lightly in one direction or another. It's as if two become one body, moving beautifully. The dance takes surrender, willingness, and attentiveness from one person and gentle guidance and skill from the other.

My eyes drew back to the word Guidance. When I saw 'G', I thought of God, followed by 'u' and 'i'. God, you, and I dance. As I lowered my head, I became willing to trust that I would get guidance about my life. Once again, I became willing to let God lead.

My prayer for you today is that God's blessings and mercies are upon you on this day and every day. May you abide in God, as God abides in you. Dance together with God; trust Him to lead and to guide you through each season of your life.

And I Hope You Dance!

Vinton & Michele Stanfield

A Great Generation

Dear Dad

A father passing by his son's bedroom was astonished to see the bed was nicely made and everything was in order. Then he saw an envelope propped up prominently on the center of the bed. It was addressed, 'Dad'. With the worst premonition, he opened the envelope and read the letter.

"Dear Dad, It is with great regret and sorrow that I'm writing to tell you I had to elope with my new girlfriend because I wanted to avoid a scene with mom and you. I've been finding real passion with Joan and she is so nice, even with all her piercings, tattoos, and her tight motorcycle clothes. It's not only the passion, Dad, she's pregnant and Joan said that we will be very happy. Even though you don't care for her as she is so much older than I, she already owns a trailer in the woods and has a stack of firewood for the whole winter. She wants to have many more children with me and that's now one of my dreams, too. Joan taught me that marijuana doesn't really hurt anyone and we'll be growing it for us and trading it with her friends for all the cocaine and ecstasy we want. In the meantime, we'll pray that science will find a cure for AIDS so Joan can get better; she sure deserves it! Don't worry Dad, I'm 16 years old now and I know how to take care of myself.

PS: Dad, none of the above is true. I'm over at the neighbor's house. I just wanted to remind you that there are worse things in life than my report card that's in my desk center drawer. I love you! Call when it is safe for me to come home."

Vinton & Michele Stanfield

Working with the Bees

Dear God

I'm writing to say I'm sorry
For being angry yesterday.
You seemed to ignore my prayer
And things didn't go my way.

First, my car broke down
I was very late for work.
But I missed that awful accident
Was that your handiwork?

I found a house I loved
But others got there first.
I was angry, then relieved
When I heard the pipes had burst!

Yesterday, I found the perfect dress
But the color was too pale.
Today, I found the dress in red
Would You believe it was on sale!

I know You're watching over me
And I'm feeling truly blessed.
For no matter what I pray
You always know what's best!

I have this circle of E-mail friends
Who mean the world to me.
Some days I 'send' and 'send'
At other times, I let them be.

When I see each name downloaded
And view the message they've sent.

I know they've thought of me that day
And 'well wishes' were their intent.

I am so blessed to have these friends
With whom I've grown so close.
So this little poem I dedicate to them
Because, to me, they are the 'Most'!

So to you, my friends, I would like to say
Thank you for being a part,
Of all my daily contacts.
This comes right from my heart.

God bless you all, is my prayer today,
I'm honored to call you friend.
I pray the Lord will keep you safe
Until we write again.

DEATH

WHAT A WONDERFUL WAY TO EXPLAIN IT…

A sick man turned to his doctor as he was preparing to leave the examination room and said, "Doctor, I am afraid to die. Tell me what lies on the other side." Very quietly, the doctor said, "I don't know." "You don't know? You, a Christian man, do not know what is on the other side?"

The doctor was holding the handle of the door. On the other side came a sound of scratching and whining, and as he opened the door, a dog sprang into the room and leaped on him with an eager show of gladness.

Turning to the patient, the doctor said, "Did you notice my dog? He's never been in this room before now. He didn't know what was inside. He knew nothing except that his master was here, and when the door opened, he sprang in without fear.

I know little of what is on the other side of death, but I do know one thing. I know my Master is there and that is enough."

Vinton & Michele Stanfield

The Next Greatest Generation

This is one of the funniest, most well-written pieces I've seen in awhile. It had me rolling on the floor laughing but please note that the author says he is from Kansas... NOT Texas. We apparently do not have a corner on the market of stupid.

Deer Rop'in

I had this idea that I was going to rope a deer, put it in a stall, feed it up on corn for a couple of weeks, then kill it and eat it.

The first step in this adventure was getting a deer. I figured that since they congregate at my cattle feeder and do not seem to have much fear of me when we are there, (a bold one will sometimes come right up and sniff at the bags of feed while I am in the back of the truck not four feet away) that it should not be difficult to rope one, get up to it and toss a bag over its head (to calm it down) then hog tie it and transport it home.

I filled the cattle feeder then hid down at the end with my rope. The cattle, which had seen the roping thing before, stayed well back. They were not having any of it.

After about twenty minutes my deer appeared, three of them. I picked out a likely looking one, stepped out from the end of the feeder and threw my rope. The deer just stood there and stared at me. I wrapped the rope around my waist and twisted the end so I would have a good hold. The deer still just stood and stared at me, but you could tell it was mildly intrigued about the whole rope situation. I took a step towards it. It took a step away. I put a little tension on the rope and received an education.

The first thing that I learned is, that while deer may just stand there looking at you funny while you attempt to rope it, they are spurred to action when you start pulling on that rope. That deer EXPLODED!

The second thing I learned is that, pound for pound, a deer is a LOT stronger than a cow or a colt. A cow or a colt in that weight range I could fight down with a rope with some dignity. A deer... no chance. That thing ran and bucked and twisted and pulled. There was no controlling it and certainly no getting close to it.

As it jerked me off my feet and started dragging me across the ground, it occurred to me that having a deer on a rope was not nearly as good an idea as I originally imagined. The only up-side is that they do not have as much stamina as many animals. A brief ten minutes later, it was tired and not nearly as quick to jerk me and drag me when I managed to get up on my feet. It took me a few minutes to realize this, since I was mostly blinded by the blood flowing out of the big gash in my head.

At that point I had lost my taste for corn fed venison and I just wanted to get that devil creature off the end of the rope. I figured if I just let it go with the rope hanging around its neck, it would likely die slow and painfully somewhere. At the time, there was no love at all between me and that deer.

I hated the thing and I would venture a guess that the feeling was mutual. Despite the gash in my head and the several large knots, where I had cleverly arrested the deer's momentum by bracing my head against various large rocks as it dragged me across the ground, I could still think clearly enough to recognize that there was a small chance that I shared some tiny amount of responsibility for the situation and I didn't want the deer to have to suffer a slow death. I managed to get it lined up to back in between my truck and the feeder, a little trap I had set beforehand, kind of like a squeeze chute. I got it to back in there and started moving up so I could get the rope.

Did you know that deer bite? They do! I never in a million years would have thought that a deer would bite somebody and so I was very surprised when I reached up there to grab that rope and the deer grabbed hold of my wrist. Now, when a deer bites you, it is not like being bit by a horse where they just bite you and then let go. A deer bites you and shakes its head almost like a pit bull. They bite HARD and it hurts. The proper thing to do when a deer bites you is probably to freeze and draw back slowly. I tried screaming and shaking instead. My method was ineffective.

It seems like the deer was biting and shaking for several minutes, but it was likely only several seconds. I, being smarter than a deer (though you may be questioning that claim by now) tricked it. While I kept it busy tearing the hound out of my right arm, I reached up with my left hand and pulled that rope loose.

That was when I got my final lesson in deer behavior for the day. Deer will strike at you with their front feet. They rear right up on their back legs and strike right about head and shoulder level, and their hooves are surprisingly sharp. I learned a long time ago that when an animal like a horse strikes at you with their hooves and you can't get away easily, the best thing to do is try to make a loud noise and make an aggressive move towards the animal. This will usually cause them to back down a bit so you can escape. This was not a horse. This was a deer, so obviously such trickery would not work. In the course of a millisecond I devised a different strategy. I screamed like a woman and tried to turn and run. The reason I had always been told NOT to try to turn and run from a horse that paws at you is that there is a good chance that it will hit you in the back of the head. Deer may not be so different from horses. Besides being twice as strong and three times as evil, the second I turned to run, it hit me right in the back of the head and knocked me down.

Now when a deer paws at you and knocks you down, it doesn't immediately leave. I suspect it does not recognize that the danger has passed. What they do instead is paw your back and jump up and down on you while you are laying there crying like a little girl and covering your head. I finally managed to crawl under the truck and the deer went away.

Now, here is the local legend. I was pretty beat up. My scalp was split open, I had several large goose eggs, my wrist was bleeding pretty good and felt broken (it turned out to be just badly bruised) and my back was bleeding in a few places, though my insulated canvas jacket had protected me from the worst of it. I drove to the nearest place, which was the co-op. I got out of the truck, covered in blood and dust, looking like I'd just come from a bar-room brawl. The guy who ran the place saw me through the window and came running out yelling "what happened?" I have never seen any law in the state of Kansas that would prohibit an individual from roping a deer. I suspect that this is an area that they have overlooked entirely. Knowing, as I do, the lengths to which law enforcement personnel will go to exercise their power, I was concerned that they may find a way to twist the existing laws to paint my actions as criminal. Not wanting to admit that I had done something monumentally stupid, I told him that 'I was attacked by a deer'. I did not mention that at the time I had a rope on it.

The evidence was all over my body. Deer prints on the back of my jacket where it had stomped all over me and a large deer print on my face where it had struck me there. I asked him to call somebody to come get me. I didn't think I could make it home on my own. He did.

Later that afternoon, a game warden showed up at my house and wanted to know about the deer attack. Surprisingly, deer attacks are a rare thing and Wildlife and Parks was interested in the event. I tried to describe the attack as completely and accurately as I could. I was filling the grain hopper and this deer came out of nowhere and just started kicking the hell out of me and BIT me. It was obviously rabid or insane or something. EVERYBODY for miles around knows about the deer attack (the guy at the co-op has a big mouth).

For several weeks people dragged their kids in the house when they saw deer around and the local ranchers carried rifles when they filled their feeders. I have told several people the real story, but NEVER anybody around here. I have to see these people every day and as an outsider, a 'city folk', I have enough trouble fitting in without them snickering behind my back and whispering "there goes the dumb ____ that tried to rope the deer."

Did Jesus Use a Modem?

Did Jesus use a modem
At the Sermon on the Mount?
Did He ever try a broadcast fax
To send His message out?

Did the disciples carry beepers
As they went about their route?
Did Jesus use a modem
At the Sermon on the Mount?

Did Paul use a laptop
With lots of RAM and ROM?
Were his letters posted on email
To Paul@Rome.com?

Did the man from Macedonia
Send an e-mail saying, "Come?"
Did Paul use a laptop
With lots of RAM and ROM?

Did Moses use a joystick
At the parting of the Sea?
And a Satellite Guidance Tracking System
To show him where to be?

Did he write the law on tablets
Or are they really on CD?
Did Moses use a joystick
At the parting of the Sea?

Did Jesus really die for us
One day upon a tree?

Or was it just a hologram
Or technical wizardry?

Can you download the Live Action Video Clip
To play on your PC?
Did Jesus really die for us
One day upon a tree?

Have the wonders of this modern age
Made you question what is true?
How a single man, in a simple time
Could offer life anew?

How a sinless life, a cruel death
Then glorious life again.
Could offer more to a desperate world
Than all the inventions of man?

If, in your life, the voice of God
Is sometimes hard to hear.
With other voices calling
His doesn't touch your ear.

Then set aside your laptop and modem
And all your fancy gear.
And open your Bible, open your heart
And let your Father near.

Doesn't God Care Any More?

Sally jumped up as soon as she saw the surgeon come out of the operating room. She said, "How is my little boy? Is he going to be all right? When can I see him?" The surgeon said, "I'm sorry. We did all we could, but your boy didn't make it." Sally said, "Why do little children get cancer? Doesn't God care anymore? Where were you, God, when my son needed you?"

The surgeon asked, "Would you like some time alone with your son? One of the nurses will be out in a few minutes, before he's transported to the university." Sally asked the nurse to stay with her while she said good-bye to her son. She ran her fingers lovingly through his thick red curly hair. "Would you like a lock of his hair?" the nurse asked. Sally nodded 'yes'. The nurse cut a lock of the boy's hair, put it in a plastic bag and handed it to Sally.

The mother said, "It was Jimmy's idea to donate his body to the university, for study. He said it might help somebody else. I said "no" at first, but Jimmy said, "Mom, I won't be using it after I die. Maybe it will help some other little boy spend one more day with his Mom." She went on, "My Jimmy had a heart of gold, always thinking of someone else and always wanting to help others if he could."

Sally walked out of Children's Mercy Hospital for the last time, after spending most of the last six months there. She put the bag with Jimmy's belongings on the seat beside her in the car. The drive home was difficult. It was even harder to enter the empty house.

She carried Jimmy's belongings and the plastic bag with the lock of his hair to her son's room. She started placing the model cars and other personal things back in his room exactly where he had always kept them. She lay down across his bed and, hugging his pillow, cried herself to sleep.

It was around midnight when Sally awoke. Lying beside her on the bed was a folded letter. The letter said:

"Dear Mom, I know you're going to miss me but don't think that I will ever forget you, or stop loving you, just because I'm not around to say 'I LOVE YOU'. I will always love you, Mom, even more with each day. Someday we will see each other again. Until then, if you want to adopt a little boy so you won't be so lonely, that's okay with me.

He can have my room and old stuff to play, but, if you decide to get a girl instead, she probably wouldn't like the same things boys do. You'll have to buy her dolls and stuff girls like, you know. Don't be sad thinking about me. This really is a neat place. Grandma and Grandpa met me as soon as I got here and showed me around some, but it will take a long time to see everything.

The angels are so cool. I love to watch them fly. And, you know what? Jesus doesn't look like any of his pictures. Yet, when I saw Him, I knew it was Him. Jesus, Himself, took me to see GOD! And guess what, Mom? I got to sit on God's knee and talk to Him, like I was somebody important. That's when I told Him that I wanted to write you a letter, to tell you good-bye and everything even though I already knew that wasn't allowed.

Well, you know what Mom? God handed me some paper and His own personal pen to write you this letter. I think Gabriel is the name of the angel who is going to drop this letter off to you. God said for me to give you the answer to one of the questions you asked Him "Where was He when I needed him?"

God said He was in the same place with me, as when His Son, Jesus, was on the cross. He was right there, as He always is with all His children.

Oh, by the way, Mom, no one else can see what I've written except you. To everyone else this is just a blank piece of paper. Isn't that cool? I have to give God His pen back now. He needs it to write some more names in the Book of Life.

Tonight I get to sit at the table with Jesus for supper. I'm sure the food will be great.

Oh, I almost forgot to tell you. I don't hurt anymore. The cancer is all gone. I'm glad because I couldn't stand that pain anymore and God couldn't stand to see me hurt so much, either. That's when He sent The Angel of Mercy to come get me. The Angel said I was a Special Delivery! How about that?"

Signed with Love from:

God, Jesus & Me

"We can't go swimming, Poppa's fishing."

For You

I wish for you...

Comfort on difficult days,
Smiles when sadness intrudes,
Rainbows to follow the clouds,
Laughter to kiss your lips,
Sunsets to warm your heart,
Gentle hugs when spirits sag,
Friendships to brighten your being,
Beauty for your eyes to see,
Confidence for when you doubt,
Faith so that you can believe,
Courage to know yourself,
Patience to accept the truth,
And love to complete your life.

God Bless you!

I asked the Lord to bless you
As I prayed for you today,
To guide you and protect you
As you go along your way.

His love is always with you

His promises are true.

No matter what the tribulation

You know He will see us through.

So when, on the road you're traveling,

Seems difficult at best.

Give your problems to the Lord

And He will do the rest.

Friends Are
God's Way of Taking Care of Us

This was written by a Hospice of Metro Denver physician.

I just had one of the most amazing experiences of my life, and wanted to share it with my family and friends.

I was driving home from a meeting this evening about five o'clock, stuck in traffic on Colorado Boulevard, and the car started to choke and splutter and die. I barely managed to coast, cursing, into a gas station, glad only that I would not be blocking traffic and would have a somewhat warm spot to wait for the tow truck. The car wouldn't start. Before I could make the call, I saw a woman walking out of the 'quickie mart' and it looked like she slipped on some ice and fell into a gas pump. So, I got out to see if she was okay. When I got there, it looked more like she had been overcome by sobs than that she had fallen. She was a young woman who looked really haggard with dark circles under her eyes. She dropped something as I helped her up and I picked it up to give it to her. It was a nickel.

At that moment, everything came into focus for me: the crying woman, the ancient Suburban crammed full of stuff with three kids in the back (one in a car seat), and the gas pump reading $4.95. I asked her if she was okay and if she needed help. She just kept saying "I don't want my kids to see me crying," so we stood on the other side of the pump away from her car. She said she was driving to California and that things were very hard for her right now. So I asked, "And you were praying?" That made her back away from me a little, but I assured her I was not a crazy person and said, "He heard you, and He sent me."

I took out my card and swiped it through the card reader on the pump so she could fill up her car completely, and while it was fueling walked to the next door McDonald's and bought two big bags of food, some gift certificates for more, and a big cup of coffee. She gave the food to the kids in the car, who attacked it like wolves, and we stood by the pump eating fries and talking a little.

She told me her name and that she lived in Kansas City. Her boyfriend left two months ago and she had not been able to make ends meet. She knew she wouldn't have money to pay rent come the first of January. Finally, in desperation she had called her parents with whom she had not spoken to in about five years. They lived in California and said she could come live with them and try to get her on her feet. So she packed up everything she owned in the car. She told the kids they were going to California for Christmas but not that they were going to live there.

I gave her my gloves, a little hug and said a quick prayer with her for safety on the road. As I was walking over to my car, she said, "So, are you like an angel or something?" This definitely made me cry. I said, "Sweetie, at this time of year angels are really busy, so sometimes God uses regular people to do what needs to be done."

It was so incredible to be a part of someone else's miracle. And of course, you guessed it, when I got in my car it started right away and got me home with no problem. I will put it in the shop tomorrow but I suspect the mechanic won't find anything wrong.

Sometimes the angels fly close enough to you that you can hear the flutter of their wings.

Psalms 55:22 "Cast thy burden upon the Lord, and He shall sustain thee. He shall never suffer the righteous to be moved."

This prayer is powerful and prayer is one of the best gifts we receive. There is no cost but a lot of rewards, let's continue to pray for one another.

Here is the prayer:

"Father, I ask You to bless my children, grandchildren, relatives and friends reading this right now. Show them a new revelation of Your love and power. Holy Spirit, I ask You to minister to their spirit at this very moment. Where there is pain, give them Your peace and mercy. Where there is self doubt, release a renewed confidence through Your grace, in Jesus' precious name. Amen."

Retired and a 'Wanna Be'

Friends

I have a list of folks I know....all written in a book,
and every now and then....I go and take a look.
That is when I realize...these names, they are a part,
not only in the book they're written...but taken from the heart.

For each name stands for someone...who has crossed my
path sometime, and in that meeting they have become...the
reason and the rhyme.

Although it sounds fantastic...for me to make this claim,
I really am composed...of each remembered name.

Although you're not aware...of any special link,
just knowing you has shaped my life....more than you could
think. So please don't think my greeting...as just a mere
routine, your name was not...forgotten in between.

For when I send a greeting....that is addressed to you,
it is because you're on the list...of folks I'm indebted to.

So whether I have known you......for many days or few,
in some ways you have a part......in shaping things I do.

I am but a total...of many folks I've met,
you are a friend I would prefer....never to forget.

Thank you for being my friend!

Vinton & Michele Stanfield

Friends in Our Lives

Friendship

One day, when I was a freshman in high school, I noticed a kid from my class walking home from school. His name was Kyle and it looked like he was carrying all of his books. I thought to myself, *"Why would anyone bring home all his books on a Friday? He must really be a nerd."* I had quite a weekend planned (parties and a football game with my friends on Saturday afternoon), so I shrugged my shoulders and continued on my way. As I was walking, I saw a bunch of kids running toward him. To my surprise, they ran at him, knocking all his books out of his arms and tripping him so he landed in the dirt. His glasses went flying and I saw them land in the grass about ten feet from him. He looked up and I saw this terrible sadness in his eyes. My heart went out to him as I jogged in his direction. He crawled around looking for his glasses and I saw tears in his eyes. As I handed him his glasses, I said, "Those guys are jerks. They really should get lives." He looked at me and said, "Hey thanks!" There was a big smile on his face. It was one of those smiles that showed real gratitude.

I helped him pick up his books and asked him where he lived. As it turned out, he lived near me, so I asked him why I had never seen him before. He said he had gone to private school before now. I would have never hung out with a private school kid but we talked all the way home and I carried some of his books. He turned out to be a pretty cool kid. I asked him if he wanted to play a little football with my friends. He said 'yes'. We hung out all weekend and the more I got to know Kyle, the more I liked him, and my friends thought the same of him. Monday morning came and there was Kyle with the huge stack of books again. I stopped him and said, "Boy, you are going to really build some serious muscles with this pile of books everyday!" He just laughed and handed me half the books.

Over the next four years, Kyle and I became best friends. When we were seniors, we began to think about college. Kyle decided on Georgetown and I planned to go to Duke. I knew that we would always be friends and that the miles would never be a problem. He was going to be a doctor and I was going for business on a football scholarship.

Kyle was valedictorian of our class. I teased him all the time about being a nerd. He had to prepare a speech for graduation. I was so glad it wasn't me having to get up there and speak. On Graduation day, I saw Kyle and he looked great. He was one of those guys that really found himself during high school. He filled out and actually looked good in glasses. He had more dates than I had and all the girls loved him. Boy, sometimes I was jealous. Today was one of those days. I could see that he was nervous about his speech. So, I smacked him on the back and said, "Hey", I began, "Graduation is a time to thank those who helped you make it through those tough years; your parents, your teachers, your siblings, maybe a coach...but mostly your friends," I joked.

I was rather surprised when Kyle began his speech and said, "I am here to tell all of you that being a friend to someone is the best gift you can give to them. I am going to tell you a story." I just looked at my friend with disbelief as he told the story of the first day we met. He had planned to kill himself over the weekend. He talked of how he had cleaned out his locker so his Mom wouldn't have to do it later and was carrying his stuff home. He looked hard at me and gave me a little smile. "Thankfully, I was saved. My friend saved me from doing the unspeakable." I heard the gasp go through the crowd as this handsome, popular boy told us all about his weakest moment. I saw his Mom and Dad looking at me and smiling that same grateful smile. Not until that moment did I realize its depth.

Never underestimate the power of your actions. With one small gesture you can change a person's life for better or for worse. God puts us all in each other's lives to impact one another in some way. Look for God in others. Friends are angels who lift us to our feet when our wings have trouble remembering how to fly. There is no beginning or end. Yesterday is history. Tomorrow is mystery. Today is a gift.

Idaho Family Reunion

Funny Isn't It?

Funny how a $100 looks so big when you take it to church but it is so small when you take it to the mall.

Funny how long it takes to serve God for an hour but how quickly a team plays 60 minutes of basketball.

Funny how long a couple of hours are spent at church but how short they are when watching a movie.

Funny how we can't think of anything to say when we pray but don't have difficulty thinking of things to talk about to a friend.

Funny how we get thrilled when a baseball game goes into extra innings but we complain when a sermon is longer than the regular time.

Funny how hard it is to read a chapter in the Bible but how easy it is to read 100 pages of a best-selling novel.

Funny how people want to get a front seat at any game or concert but they scramble to get a back seat at church services.

Funny how we need 2 or 3 weeks advance notice to fit a church event into our schedule but can adjust our time for other events at the last moment.

Funny how hard it is for people to learn a simple gospel well enough to tell others but how simple it is for the same people to understand and repeat gossip.

Funny how we believe what appears in the newspaper but we question what appears in the Bible.

Funny how everyone wants to go to Heaven provided they do not have to believe, think, say, or do anything.

Funny how you can send a thousand 'jokes' through e-mail and they spread like wildfire but when you start sending messages regarding the Lord, people think twice about sharing.

FUNNY, ISN'T IT? Are you laughing? Are you thinking?

Spread the Word and give thanks to the Lord for He is good!

God in High School

This is a statement that was read over the public address system, on September 1, 2000, at the football game at Roane County High School, Kingston, Tennessee, by school Principal, Jody McLeod.

"It has always been the custom at Roane County High School football games, to say a prayer and play the National Anthem, to honor God and Country.

Due to a recent ruling by the Supreme Court, I am told that saying a prayer is a violation of Federal Case Law. As I understand the law at this time, I can use this public facility to approve of sexual perversion and call it 'an alternate lifestyle' and if someone is offended, that's OK. I can use it to condone sexual promiscuity, by dispensing condoms and calling it 'safe sex' and if someone is offended, that's OK. I can even use this public facility to present the merits of killing an unborn baby as a 'viable means of birth control' and if someone is offended, no problem. I can designate a school day as 'Earth Day' and involve students in activities to worship religiously and praise the goddess 'Mother Earth' and call it 'ecology'. I can use literature, videos and presentations in the classroom that depict people with strong, traditional Christian convictions as 'simple minded and ignorant' and call it 'enlightenment'.

However, if anyone uses this facility to honor GOD and to ask HIM to bless this event with safety and good sportsmanship, then Federal Case Law is violated. This appears to be inconsistent at best, and at worst, diabolical. Apparently, we are to be tolerant of everything and anyone, except GOD and HIS Commandments. Nevertheless, as a school principal, I frequently ask staff and students to abide by rules with which they do not necessarily agree. For me to do otherwise would be inconsistent at best, and at worst, would be hypocritical. I suffer from that affliction enough unintentionally. I certainly do not need to add an intentional transgression. For this reason, I shall 'Render unto Caesar that which is Caesar's and refrain from praying at this time.

However, if you feel inspired to honor, praise and thank GOD and ask HIM, in the name of JESUS, to bless this event, please feel free to do so. As far as I know, that's not against the law - yet. One by one, the people in the stands bowed their heads, held hands with one another and began to pray. They prayed in the stands. They prayed in the team huddles. They prayed at the concession stand and they prayed in the announcer's box.

The only place they didn't pray was in the Supreme Court of the United States of America - the seat of 'justice' in the "one nation, under GOD."

Somehow, Kingston, Tennessee remembered what so many have forgotten. We are given the Freedom of Religion, not the Freedom _FROM_ Religion. Praise GOD that HIS remnant remains.

JESUS said, "If you are ashamed of ME before men, then I will be ashamed of you before MY FATHER."- Matthew 10:32.

God in the Grocery Store

Louise Redden, a poorly dressed lady, with a look of defeat on her face, walked into a grocery store. She approached the owner of the store in a most humble manner and asked if he would let her charge a few groceries. She softly explained that her husband was very ill and unable to work, they had seven children and they needed food. John Longhouse, the grocer, scoffed at her and requested that she leave his store. Visualizing the family needs, she said, "Please, sir! I will bring you the money just as soon as I can." John told her he could not give her credit as she did not have a charge account at his store.

Standing beside the counter was a customer who overheard the conversation between the two. He walked forward and told the grocer that he would stand good for whatever she needed for her family. The grocer said in a very reluctant voice, "Do you have a grocery list?" Louise replied, "Yes sir." "O.K.", he said, "Put your grocery list on the scales and whatever your grocery list weighs, I will give you that amount in groceries." Louise hesitated a moment with a bowed head, then she reached into her purse and took out a piece of paper and scribbled something on it. She then laid the piece of paper on the scale carefully with her head still bowed.

The grocer's and the customer's eyes showed amazement when the scales went down and stayed down. The grocer, staring at the scales, turned slowly to the customer and said begrudgingly, "I can't believe it." The customer smiled and the grocer started putting the groceries on the other side of the scales. The scale did not balance so he continued to put more and more groceries on them until the scales would hold no more. The grocer stood there in utter disgust. Finally, he grabbed the piece of paper from the scales and looked at it with greater amazement.

It was not a grocery list. It was a prayer, which said, "Dear Lord, you know my needs and I am leaving this in your hands."

The grocer gave her the groceries that he had gathered and stood in stunned silence. Louise thanked him and left the store. The customer who had volunteered to pay for the groceries handed a fifty-dollar bill to the grocer and said, "It was worth every penny of it."

God Knows Where I Am

Do you believe that God not only loves you but knows where you are and what you're doing every minute of the day? I certainly do after an amazing experience I had several years ago.

At the time I was driving on I-75 near Dayton, Ohio, with my wife and children. We turned off the highway for a rest and refreshment stop. My wife, Barbara, and children went into the restaurant. I suddenly felt the need to stretch my legs, so I waved them off ahead saying I'd join them later.

I bought a soft drink and as I walked from a Dairy Queen, feelings of self pity enshrouded my mind. I loved the Lord and my ministry but I felt drained and burdened. My cup was empty.

Suddenly, the impatient ringing of a telephone nearby jarred me out of my doldrums. It was coming from a phone booth at a service station on the corner. Wasn't anyone going to answer the phone? Noise from the traffic flowing through the busy intersection must have drowned out the sound because the service station attendant continued looking after his customers, oblivious to the incessant ringing. "Why doesn't somebody answer that phone?" I muttered. I began reasoning. It may be important. What if it's an emergency? Curiosity overcame my indifference. I stepped inside the booth and picked up the phone. "Hello," I said casually and took a big sip of my drink. The operator said, "Long distance call for Ken Gaub." My eyes widened and I almost choked on a chunk of ice.

Swallowing hard, I said, "You're crazy!" Then, realizing I shouldn't speak to an operator like that, I added, "This can't be! I was walking down the road, not bothering anyone, and the phone was ringing...." "Is Ken Gaub there?" the operator interrupted, "I have a long distance call for him." It took a moment to gain control of my babbling but I finally replied, "Yes, he is here." Searching for a possible explanation, I wondered if I could possibly be on Candid Camera!

Still shaken, perplexed, I asked, "How in the world did you reach me here? I was walking down the road, the pay phone started ringing and I just answered it by chance. You can't mean me." "Well," the operator asked, "is Mr. Gaub there or isn't he?" "Yes, I am Ken Gaub," I said, finally convinced by the tone of her voice that the call was real. Then, I heard another voice say, "Yes, that's him, operator. That's Ken Gaub."

I listened dumbfounded to a strange voice identify herself. "I'm Millie from Harrisburg, Pennsylvania. You don't know me, Mr. Gaub, but I'm desperate. Please help me." I said, "What can I do for you?" She began weeping. Finally, she regained control and continued, "I was about to commit suicide, had just finished writing a note, when I began to pray and tell God I really didn't want to do this. Then, I suddenly remembered seeing you on television and thought if I could just talk to you, you could help me. I knew that was impossible because I didn't know how to reach you. I didn't know anyone who could help me find you. Then, some numbers came to mind and I scribbled them down." At this point she began weeping again, and I prayed silently for wisdom to help her. She continued, "I looked at the numbers and thought, *Would't it be wonderful if I had a miracle from God and He has given me Ken's phone number?* I decided to try calling it. I can't believe I'm talking to you. Are you in your office in California?" I replied, "Ma'am, I don't have an office in California. My office is in Yakima, Washington." A little surprised, she asked, "Oh, really, then where are you?" "Don't you know?" I responded, "You made the call."

She explained, "But I don't even know what area I'm calling. I just dialed the number that I had on this paper." "Ma'am, you won't believe this but I'm in a phone booth in Dayton, Ohio!" "Really?" she exclaimed. "Well, what are you doing there?" I kidded her gently, "Well, I'm answering the phone. It was ringing as I walked by; so, I answered it."

Knowing this encounter could only have been arranged by God, I began to counsel the woman. As she told me of her despair and frustration, the presence of the Holy Spirit flooded the phone booth giving me words of wisdom beyond my ability. In a matter of moments, she prayed the sinner's prayer and met the One who would lead her out of her situation into a new life.

I walked away from that telephone booth with an electrifying sense of our heavenly Father's concern for each of His children. What were the astronomical odds of this happening? With all the millions of phones and innumerable combinations of numbers, only an all-knowing God could have caused that woman to call that number in that phone booth at that moment in time.

Forgetting my drink and nearly bursting with exhilaration, I headed back to my family, wondering if they would believe my story. "Maybe I had better not tell this," I thought, but I couldn't contain it. "Barb, you won't believe this. God knows where I am!"

God also knows where you are. Place yourself in His hands, concentrate on knowing His will for your life, and He will never forsake or forget you.

Ken Gaub

God Said "NO"

I asked God to take away my habit.
God said, "No. It is not for Me to take away
but for you to give it up."

I asked God to make my handicapped child whole.
God said, "No, his spirit is whole, his body is only
temporary."

I asked God to grant me patience.
God said, "No. Patience is a byproduct of tribulations.
It isn't granted, it is learned."

I asked God to give me happiness.
God said, "No. I give you blessings,
happiness is up to you."

I asked God to spare me pain.
God said, "No. Suffering draws you apart from
worldly cares and brings you closer to me."

I asked God to make my spirit grow.
God said, "No. You must grow on your own,
but I will prune you to make you fruitful."

I asked God for all things that I might enjoy life.
God said, "No. I will give you life,
so that you may enjoy all things."

I asked God to help me LOVE others,
as much as He loves me.
God said, "Ahhhh, finally you have the idea."

This day is yours, don't throw it away. May God Bless You.

*To the world you might be one person,
but to one person you just might be the world.*

*May the Lord Bless you and keep you.
May the Lord make His face shine upon you,
And give you Peace...Forever.*

*Good friends are like stars.
You don't always see them
but you know they are always there.*

God's Thoughts on Lawns

GOD: "Frank, you know all about gardens and nature. What in the world is going on down there on the planet? What happened to the dandelions, violets, thistles and stuff I started eons ago? I had a perfect, no-maintenance garden plan. Those plants grow in any type of soil, withstand drought and multiply with abandon. The nectar from the long lasting blossoms attracts butterflies, honey bees and flocks of songbirds. I expected to see a vast garden of colors by now but all I see are these green rectangles."

ST. FRANCIS: "It's the tribes that settled there, Lord, the Suburbanites. They started calling your flowers 'weeds' and went to great lengths to kill them and replace them with grass."

GOD: "Grass? But it's so boring. It's not colorful. It doesn't attract butterflies, birds and bees, only grubs and sod worms. It's sensitive to temperatures. Do these Suburbanites really want all that grass growing there?"

ST. FRANCIS: "Apparently so, Lord. They go to great pains to grow it and keep it green. They begin each spring by fertilizing grass and poisoning any other plant that crops up in the lawn."

GOD: "The spring rains and warm weather probably make grass grow really fast. That must make the Suburbanites happy."

ST. FRANCIS: "Apparently not, Lord. As soon as it grows a little, they cut it -- sometimes twice a week."

GOD: "They cut it? Do they then bail it like hay?"

ST. FRANCIS: "Not exactly, Lord. Most of them rake it up and put it in bags."

GOD: "They bag it? Why? Is it a cash crop? Do they sell it?"

ST. FRANCIS: "No Sir, just the opposite. They pay to throw it away."

GOD: "Now let me get this straight. They fertilize grass so it will grow and when it does grow they cut it and pay to throw it away?"

ST. FRANCIS: "Yes, Sir."

GOD: "These Suburbanites must be relieved in the summer when we cut back on the rain and turn up the heat. That surely slows the growth and saves them a lot of work".

ST. FRANCIS: "You aren't going to believe this Lord. When the grass stops growing so fast, they drag out hoses and pay more money to water it so they can continue to mow it and pay to get rid of it."

GOD: "What nonsense! At least they kept some of the trees. That was a sheer stroke of genius, if I do say so myself. The trees grow leaves in the spring to provide beauty and shade in the summer. In the autumn the leaves fall to the ground and form a natural blanket to keep moisture in the soil and protect the trees and bushes. Plus, as they rot, the leaves form compost to enhance the soil. It's a natural circle of life."

ST. FRANCIS: "You better sit down, Lord. The Suburbanites have drawn a new circle. As soon as the leaves fall, they rake them into great piles and pay to have them hauled away."

GOD: "No. What do they do to protect the shrub and tree roots in the winter and to keep the soil moist and loose?"

ST. FRANCIS: "After throwing away the leaves, they go out and buy something which they call mulch. They haul it home and spread it around in place of the leaves."

GOD: "And where do they get this mulch?"

ST. FRANCIS: "They cut down trees and grind them up to make the mulch."

GOD: "Enough! I don't want to think about this anymore. St. Catherine, you're in charge of the arts. What movie have you scheduled for us tonight?"

ST. CATHERINE: "*Dumb and Dumber*, Lord. It's a real stupid movie about..."

GOD: "Never mind, I think I just heard the whole story from St. Francis."

This Sign Says It All!

Great Truths

That Little Children Have Learned:

1. No matter how hard you try, you can't baptize cats.
2. When your mom is mad at your dad, don't let her brush your hair.
3. If your sister hits you, don't hit her back. They always catch the second person.
4. Never ask your 3-year old brother to hold a tomato.
5. You can't trust dogs to watch your food.
6. Don't sneeze when someone is cutting your hair.
7. Never hold a dust-buster and a cat at the same time.
8. You can't hide a piece of broccoli in a glass of milk.
9. Don't wear polka-dot underwear under white shorts.
10. The best place to be when you're sad is Grandpa's lap.

That Adults Have Learned:

1. Raising teenagers is like nailing jelly to a tree.
2. Wrinkles don't hurt.
3. Families are like fudge...mostly sweet, with a few nuts.
4. Today's mighty oak is just yesterday's nut that held its ground.
5. Laughing is good exercise. It's like jogging on the inside.
6. Middle age is when you choose your cereal for the fiber and not the toy.

About Growing Old:

1. Growing old is mandatory; growing up is optional.
2. Forget the health food. I need all the preservatives I can get.

3. When you fall down, you wonder what else you can do while you're down there.
4. You're getting old when you get the same sensation from a rocking chair that you once got from a roller coaster.
5. It is frustrating when you know all the answers but nobody bothers to ask you the questions.
6. Time may be a great healer but it's a lousy beautician.
7. Wisdom comes with age but sometimes age comes alone.

The Four Stages of Life

1. You believe in Santa Claus.
2. You don't believe in Santa Claus.
3. You are Santa Claus.
4. You look like Santa Claus.

SUCCESS
At age 4 success is…not peeing in your pants.
At age 12 success is…having friends.
At age 17 success is…having a driver's license.
At age 35 success is…having money.
At age 50 success is…having money.
At age 70 success is…having a driver's license.
At age 75 success is…having friends.
At age 80 success is…not peeing in your pants.

Try to forget the troubles that pass your way but never forget the blessings that come each day.

Age does not protect you from love; but love, to some extent, protects you from age.

Guide to a Good Life

Give people more than they expect and do it cheerfully.

Marry a man/woman with whom you love to talk. As you get older, their conversational skills will be as important as any other.

Don't believe all you hear, spend all you have, or sleep all you want.

When you say, "I love you," mean it.

When you say, "I'm sorry," look the person in the eye.

Be engaged at least six months before you get married.

Believe in love at first sight.

Never laugh at anyone's dream. People who don't have dreams don't have much.

Love deeply and passionately. You might get hurt but it's the only way to live life completely.

In disagreements, fight fairly. No name calling.

Don't judge people by their relatives.

Talk slowly but think quickly.

When someone asks you a question you don't want to answer, smile and ask, "Why do you want to know?"

Remember that great love and great achievements involve great risk.

Say "bless you" when you hear someone sneeze.

When you lose, don't lose the lesson.

Remember the three R's: Respect for self; Respect for others; and Responsibility for all your actions.

Don't let a little dispute injure a great friendship.

When you realize you've made a mistake, take immediate steps to correct it.

Smile, when picking up the phone. The caller will hear it in your voice.

Spend some time alone.

Have You Tasted My Jesus?

At the University of Chicago Divinity School each year they have what is called 'Baptist Day'. It is a day when all the Baptists in the area are invited to the school. On this day each one is to bring a lunch to be eaten outdoors in a grassy picnic area. Every 'Baptist Day', the school would invite one of the greatest minds to lecture in the theological education center.

One year they invited Dr. Paul Tillich. Dr. Tillich spoke for two and one-half hours attempting to prove that the Resurrection of Jesus was false. He quoted scholar after scholar and book after book. He concluded that since there was no such thing as the historical resurrection the religious tradition of the church was groundless and emotional mumbo-jumbo. He said it was based on a relationship with a risen Jesus, who, in fact, never rose from the dead in any literal sense. He then asked if there were any questions. After about 30 seconds, an old, dark skinned preacher with a head of short-cropped, woolly white hair stood up in the back of the auditorium.

"Doctor Tillich, I got one question," he said as all eyes turned toward him. He reached into his sack lunch and pulled out an apple and began eating it. "Doctor Tillich, (CRUNCH, MUNCH). My question is a simple question (CRUNCH, MUNCH). Now, I ain't never read them books you read (CRUNCH, MUNCH), and I can't recite the Scriptures in the original Greek (CRUNCH, MUNCH). I don't know nothin' about Niebuhr and Heidegger"

CRUNCH, MUNCH). He finished the apple. "All I wanna know, is this apple I just ate…was it bitter or sweet?"

Dr. Tillich paused for a moment and answered in exemplary scholarly fashion. "I cannot possibly answer that question for I haven't tasted your apple". The white-haired preacher dropped the core of his apple into his crumpled paper bag, looked up at Dr. Tillich and said calmly, "Neither have you tasted my Jesus."

The 1,000 plus in attendance could not contain themselves. The auditorium erupted with applause and cheers. Dr. Tillich thanked his audience and promptly left the platform.

Have you tasted Jesus? God has risen…and he's coming back one day! Taste and see that the LORD is good; blessed is the man who takes refuge in Him. If you have, rejoice in the hope of the resurrection that your faith in Him brings. Psalm 34: 8

Having Mom Over for Dinner

You don't even have to be a mother to enjoy this one.

Ben invited his mother over for dinner. During the course of the meal, she couldn't help but notice how beautiful Ben's roommate, Jennifer, was. Ben's mom had long been suspicious of the platonic relationship between Ben and Jennifer, and this had only made her more curious.

Over the course of the evening, while watching the two interact, she started to wonder if there was more between Ben and Jennifer than met the eye. Reading his mom's thoughts, Ben volunteered, "I know what you must be thinking, but I assure you Jennifer and I are just roommates."

About a week later, Jennifer came to Ben saying, "Ever since your mother came to dinner, I've been unable to find the beautiful silver gravy ladle. You don't suppose she took it, do you?" Ben said, "Well, I doubt it but I'll send her an e-mail just to be sure." So he sat down and wrote:

Dear Mom,
"I'm not saying that you 'did' take the gravy ladle from the house, I'm not saying that you 'did not' take the gravy ladle. Yet, the fact remains that one has been missing ever since you were here for dinner."
Love, Ben

Several days later, Ben received an email back from his mother that read:

Dear Son,
"I'm not saying that you 'do' sleep with Jennifer, I'm not saying that you 'do not' sleep with Jennifer. But the fact remains that if Jennifer was sleeping in her own bed, she would have found the gravy ladle by now."
Love, Mom

LESSON OF THE DAY - NEVER LIE TO YOUR MOTHER

Here in Your Heart

When tomorrow starts without me
and I'm not there to see,
If the sun should rise and find your eyes
all filled with tears for me.

I wish so much you wouldn't cry
the way you did today,
While thinking of the many things
we didn't get to say.

I know how much you love me
as much as I love you,
And each time that you think of me
I know you'll miss me too.

But when tomorrow starts without me
please try to understand,
That an angel came, called my name
and took me by the hand.

He said my place was ready in
Heaven far above,
And that I'd have to leave behind
all those things I dearly love.

Yet as I turned to walk away
a tear fell from my eye,
For all of life, I'd always thought
I didn't want to die.

I had so much to live for and

so much yet to do,
It seemed almost impossible
that I was leaving you.

I thought of all the yesterdays
the good ones and the bad,
I thought of all the love we shared
and all the fun we had.

If I could relive yesterday
just even for a while,
I'd say good-bye and kiss you
and maybe see you smile.

But then I fully realized
that it could never be,
For emptiness and memories
would take the place of me.

And when I thought of worldly things
that I might miss come tomorrow,
I thought of you and when I did
my heart was filled with sorrow.

Yet, when I walked through Heaven's gates
I felt so much at home,
When God looked down and smiled at me
from His great golden throne.

He said, "This is eternity

and all I've promised you,
Today your life on earth is past
but here it starts anew.

I promise no tomorrow
but today will always last,
And since each day's the same day
There's no longing for the past.

You have been so faithful
so trusting and so true,
Though there were times you did some things
you know you shouldn't do.

You have been forgiven
and now at last you're free,
So won't you take my hand
and share My life with Me?"

So when tomorrow starts without me
don't think we're far apart,
For every time you think of me
I'm right here in your heart.

Vinton & Michele Stanfield

"Small" Texas Reunion

Hey, Wasn't That Us?

A little house with three bedrooms, one bathroom, one car on the street, and a mower that you had to push to make the grass look neat.

In the kitchen on the wall we only had one phone, and no need for recording things as someone was always home.

We only had a living room where we would congregate, unless it was at mealtime in the kitchen where we ate.

We had no need for family rooms or extra rooms to dine, when meeting as a family those two rooms would work out fine.

We only had one TV set and channels maybe two, but always there was one of them with something worth the view.

For snacks we had potato chips that tasted like a chip, and if you wanted flavor there was Lipton's onion dip.

Store-bought snacks were rare because my mother liked to cook, and nothing can compare to snacks in Betty Crocker's book.

Weekends were for family trips or staying home to play, we all did things together even go to church to pray.

When we did our weekend trips depending on the weather, no one stayed at home because we liked to be together.

Sometimes we would separate to do things on our own, but we knew where the others were without our own cell phone.

Then there were the movies with your favorite movie star,
and nothing can compare to watching movies in your car.

There were the picnics at the peak of summer season, pack
a lunch and find some trees and never need a reason.

Get a baseball game together with all the friends you know,
have real action playing ball -- and no game video.

Remember when the doctor used to be the family friend,
and didn't need insurance or a lawyer to defend?

Remember going to the store and shopping casually, and
when you went to pay for it you used your own money?

Nothing that you had to swipe or punch in some amount,
remember, when the cashier had to really count?

The milkman used to deliver going from door to door, and
it was just a few cents more than going to the store.

There was a time when mail came right to your door,
without a lot of junk ads sent out by every store.

The mailman knew each house by name and knew where
letters were sent, and there were not loads of mail
addressed to 'local occupant'.

There was a time when just one glance was all that it would
take, and you would know the kind of car, the model and
the make.

They didn't look like turtles trying to squeeze out every
mile; they were streamlined, white walls, fins, and really
had some style.

One time the music that you played whenever you would jive, was from a vinyl, big-holed record called a forty-five.

The record player had a post to keep them all in line, and then the records would drop down and play one at a time.

Oh sure, we had our problems then, just like we do today, and always we were striving, trying for a better way.

Oh, the simple life we lived still seems like so much fun, how can you explain a game, just 'kick the can and run'?

And why would boys put baseball cards between bicycle spokes, and for a nickel a red machine had little bottled Cokes?

This life seemed so much easier and slower in some ways, I love the new technology but I sure miss those days. So time moves on, and so do we, and nothing stays the same, but I sure love to reminisce and walk down memory lane.

Thomas Tucker

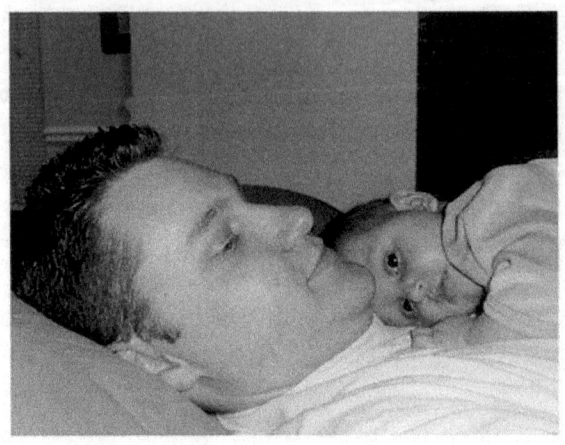

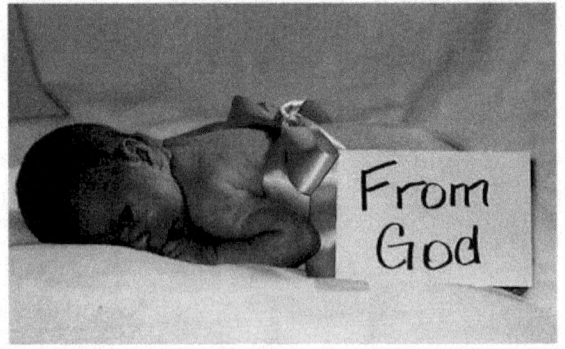

More Blessings

I Am Thankful...

For the husband who sometimes complains when his dinner is not on time because he is home with me, not somewhere else.

For the teenager who complains about doing dishes because that means she is at home and not on the streets.

For the payroll taxes that I pay because it means that I am employed.

For the mess I clean after a party because it means that I have been surrounded by friends.

For the clothes that fit a little too snug because it means I have enough to eat.

For my shadow that watches me work because it means I am out in the sunshine.

For a lawn that needs mowing, windows that need cleaning, and gutters that need fixing because it means I have a home.

For all the complaining I hear about the government because it means that we still have freedom of speech.

For the parking spot I find at the far end of the parking lot because it means I am capable of walking and that I have been blessed with transportation.

For my huge heating bill because it means I am warm.

For the lady behind me in church that sings off key because it means that I can hear.

For the pile of laundry and ironing because it means I have clothes to wear.

For weariness and aching muscles at the end of the day because it means I am capable of working hard.

For the alarm that goes off in the early morning hours because it means that I am alive.

And finally…for too much Email because it means that I have friends who are thinking of me.

I Dreamt That I Went to Heaven

I dreamt that I went to Heaven and an angel was taking me on a tour. We walked side-by-side and arrived inside a large workroom filled with angels.

My angel guide stopped in front of the first section and said, "This is the Receiving Section. Here, all petitions to God said in prayer are received." I looked around in this area. It was terribly busy with so many angels sorting out petitions written on voluminous paper sheets and scraps from people all over the world.

Then we moved on down a long corridor until we reached the second section. The angel then said to me, "This is the Packaging and Delivery Section. Here, the graces and blessings the people requested are processed and delivered to the living persons who asked for them."

I noticed again how busy it was there. There were many angels working hard at that station, since so many blessings had been requested and were being packaged for delivery to Earth.

Finally, at the farthest end of the long corridor we stopped at the door of a very small station. To my great surprise, only one angel was seated there, idly doing nothing. "This is the Acknowledgment Section," my angel friend quietly admitted to me. He seemed embarrassed. "How is that? There's no work going on here?" I asked. "So sad," the angel sighed. "After people receive the blessings that they requested, very few send back acknowledgments." "How does one acknowledge God's blessings?" I asked.

"Simple," the angel answered. "Just say, Thank you, Lord."
"What blessings should they acknowledge?" I asked.

"If you have food in the refrigerator, clothes on your back, a roof overhead and a place to sleep ... you are richer than 75% of this world. If you have money in the bank, in your wallet and spare change in a dish, you are among the top 8% of the worlds' wealthy. Also, if you woke up this morning with more health than illness.... you are more blessed than the many who will not even survive this day. If you have never experienced the fear in battle, the loneliness of imprisonment, the agony of torture, or the pangs of starvation, you are ahead of 700 million people in the world. If you can attend a church meeting without fear of harassment, arrest, torture or death ... you are envied by, and more blessed than 3 billion people in the world. If your parents are still alive and still married, you are very rare. If you can hold your head up and smile, you are not the norm, you are unique to all those in doubt and despair."

I Found Jesus There

The surgeon sat beside the boy's bed while the boy's parents sat across from him. "Tomorrow morning," the surgeon began, "I'll open up your heart..."

"You'll find Jesus there," the boy interrupted.

The surgeon looked up, annoyed. "I'll cut your heart open," he continued, "to see how much damage has been done..."

"But when you open up my heart, you'll find Jesus in there."

The surgeon looked to the parents, who sat quietly. "When I see how much damage has been done, I'll sew your heart and chest back up and I'll plan what to do next."

"But you'll find Jesus in my heart. The Bible says He lives there. The hymns all say He lives there. You'll find Him in my heart."

The surgeon had had enough. "I'll tell you what I'll find in your heart. I'll find damaged muscle, low blood supply, weakened vessels and I'll find out if I can make you well."

"You'll find Jesus there, too. He lives there."

The surgeon left. He sat in his office, recording his notes from the surgery, damaged aorta, damaged pulmonary vein, widespread muscle degeneration, no hope for transplant, no hope for cure. Therapy: painkillers and bed rest. Prognosis: here he paused, death within one year. He stopped the recorder but there was more to be said. "Why?" he asked aloud. "Why did You do this? You've put him here. You've put him in this pain and You've cursed him to an early death. Why?"

The Lord answered and said, "The boy, My lamb, was not meant for your flock for long, for he is a part of My flock, and will forever be here, in My flock, he will feel no pain, and will be comforted as you cannot imagine. His parents will one day join him here and they will know peace. My flock will continue to grow."

The surgeon's tears were hot but his anger was hotter. "You created that boy, and You created that heart. He'll be dead in months. Why?"

The Lord answered, "The boy, My lamb, shall return to My flock, for He has done his duty. I did not put My lamb with your flock to lose him but to retrieve another lost lamb." The surgeon wept.

The surgeon sat beside the boy's bed while the parents sat across from him. The boy awoke and whispered, "Did you cut open my heart?" "Yes," said the surgeon. "What did you find?" asked the boy. "I found Jesus there," said the surgeon.

I Wish for You...

Comfort on difficult days,

Smiles when sadness intrudes,

Rainbows to follow the clouds,

Laughter to kiss your lips,

Sunsets to warm your heart,

Gentle hugs when spirits sag,

Friendships to brighten your being,

Beauty for your eyes to see,

Confidence for when you doubt,

Faith so that you can believe,

Courage to know yourself,

Patience to accept the truth,

And love to complete your life.

God Bless you!
I asked the Lord to bless you
as I prayed for you today,
God guide you and protect you
As you go along your way.

His love is always with you
His promises are true,
No matter what the tribulation
You know He will see us through.

So when on the road you're traveling
Seems difficult at best,
Give your problems to the Lord
And God will do the rest.

I Wished I Were You

When I was a child I was always unhappy being me. It was you I wanted to be.

One day, my wish came true. I became you and you became me.

I knew I was you but you did not know you were me. You thought you were you.

Soon I discovered that I was much more unhappy being you than I ever was being me.

I wanted to go back to being me but you did not know you were me. You thought you were you.

I could not go back to being me because of you.

And now I am forever trapped being you, and am much more unhappy than I ever was BEING ME.

Eugene Humphrey

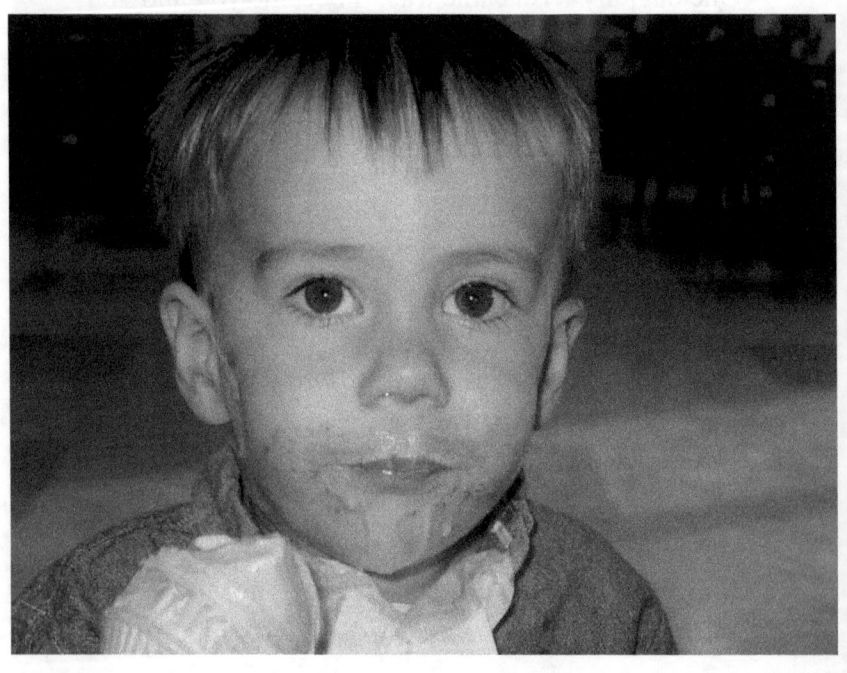

"But I didn't get any on my shirt."

Ice Cream for the Soul

Last week, I took my children to a restaurant. My six-year-old son asked if he could say grace. As we bowed our heads, he said, "God is good. God is great. Thank you for the food, and I would even thank you more if Mom gets us ice cream for dessert…and Liberty and Justice for all. Amen!"

Along with the laughter from the other customers nearby, I heard a woman remark, "That's what's wrong with this country. Kids today don't even know how to pray asking God for ice cream! Why, I never!"

Hearing this, my son burst into tears and asked me, "Did I do it wrong? Is God mad at me?" As I held him and assured him that he had done a terrific job and God was certainly not mad at him, an elderly gentleman approached the table.

He winked at my son and said, "I happen to know that God thought that was a great prayer." "Really?" my son asked. "Cross my heart." Then in theatrical whisper he added (indicating the woman whose remark had started this whole thing), "Too bad she never asks God for ice cream. A little ice cream is good for the soul sometimes."

Naturally, I bought the children ice cream at the end of the meal. My son stared at his for a moment and then did something I will remember the rest of my life. He picked up his sundae and without a word walked over and placed it in front of the woman. With a big smile he told her, "Here, this is for you. Ice cream is good for the soul sometimes and my soul is good already."

Dear Dad,

I came across this years ago. It reflects much of your life and what it has meant to me, personally. Although it is advice from a father to his son, I think it really speaks to my heart about you.

If

If you can keep your head when all about you are losing theirs and blaming it on you;
If you can trust yourself when all men doubt you and make allowance for their doubting, too.

If you can wait and not be tired of waiting, or being lied about, don't deal in lies;
Or being hated, don't give way to hating; and yet don't look too good or talk too wise.

If you can dream and not make dreams your master, if you can think and not make thoughts your aim;
If you can meet with triumph and disaster and treat these two imposters just the same.

If you can bear to hear the truth you've spoken twisted by knaves to make a trap for fools;
Or watch the things you gave your life to, broken, and stoop and build them up with worn-out tools.

If you can make one heap of all your winnings and risk it on one turn of pitch and toss,

And lose, and start again at your beginnings and never breathe a word about your loss.

If you can force your heart, nerve and sinew, to serve your turn long after they are gone;
And so hold on when there is nothing in you, except the will which says to them, "Hold on."

If you can talk with crowds and keep your virtue or walk with kings, nor lose the common touch;
If neither foes nor loving friends can hurt you, if all men count with you, but none too much.

If you can fill the unforgiving minute, worth of sixty seconds of distance run;
Then yours is the earth and everything in it and what's more, you'll be a Man, my son!
Rudyard Kipling

"For God so loved the world that He gave His only begotten Son, that whoever believes in Him, will not perish, but have everlasting life." - John 3:16

If I Knew

If I knew it would be the last time
that I'd see you fall asleep,
I would tuck you in more tightly
and pray the Lord, your soul to keep.

If I knew it would be the last time
that I see you walk out the door,
I would give you a hug and kiss
and call you back for one more.

If I knew it would be the last time
I'd hear your voice lifted up in praise,
I would video tape each action and word
so I could play them back day after day.

If I knew it would be the last time
I could spare an extra minute,
to stop and say "I love you"
instead of assuming you would know I do.

If I knew it would be the last time
I would be there to share your day,
Well I'm sure you'll have so many more
so I can let just this one slip away.

For surely there's always tomorrow
to make up for an oversight,
and we always get a second chance
to make everything just right.

There will always be another day
to say "I love you,"
And certainly there's another chance
to say our "Anything I can do?"

Just in case I might be wrong,
and today is all I get,
I'd like to say how much I love you
and I hope you never forget.

Tomorrow is not promised to anyone
young or old alike,
And today may be the last chance
you get to hold your loved one tight.

So if you're waiting for tomorrow
why not do it today?
For if tomorrow never comes
You'll surely regret the day.

That you didn't take that extra time
for a smile, a hug, or a kiss,
and you were too busy to grant someone
what turned out to be their one last wish.

So hold your loved ones close today
and whisper in their ear,
Tell them how much you love them
and that you'll always hold them dear.

Take time to say "I'm sorry",
"Please forgive me", "Thank you", or "It's okay."
And if tomorrow never comes,
you'll have no regrets about today.

I've Learned

I've learned...that the best classroom in the world is at the feet of an elderly person.

I've learned...that when you're in love, it shows.

I've learned...that just one person saying to me, "You've made my day!" makes my day.

I've learned...that having a child fall asleep in your arms is one of the most peaceful feelings in the world.

I've learned...that being kind is more important than being right.

I've learned...that you should never say "No" to a gift from a child.

I've learned...that I can always pray for someone when I don't have the strength to help him in some other way.

I've learned...that no matter how serious your life requires you to be, everyone needs a friend with whom to act goofy.

I've learned...that sometimes all a person needs is a hand to hold and a heart to understand.

I've learned...that simple walks with my father around the block on summer nights when I was a child did wonders for me as an adult.

I've learned...that life is like a roll of toilet paper. The closer it gets to the end the faster it goes!

I've learned...that we should be glad God doesn't give us everything for which we ask.

I've learned...that money doesn't buy class.

I've learned...that it's those small daily happenings that make life so spectacular.

I've learned...that under everyone's hard shell is someone who wants to be appreciated and loved.

I've learned...that if the Lord didn't do it all in one day, what makes me think I can?

I've learned...that to ignore the facts does not change the facts.

I've learned...that when you plan to get even with someone, you are only letting that person continue to hurt you.

I've learned...that love, not time, heals all wounds.

I've learned...that the easiest way for me to grow as a person is to surround myself with people smarter than I am.

I've learned...that everyone you meet deserves to be greeted with a smile.

I've learned...that there's nothing sweeter than sleeping with your babies and feeling their breath on your cheeks.

I've learned...that no one is perfect until you fall in love with them.

I've learned...that life is tough but I'm tougher.

I've learned...that those opportunities are never lost and that someone will take the ones you miss.

I've learned...that when you harbor bitterness, happiness will dock elsewhere.

I've learned...that I wish I could have told my Mom that I love her, one more time, before she passed away.

I've learned...that one should keep his words both soft and tender because tomorrow he may have to eat them.

I've learned...that a smile is an inexpensive way to improve your looks.

I've learned...that I can't choose how I feel but I can choose what I do about it.

I've learned...that when your newly born grandchild holds your little finger in their little fist, that you're hooked for life.

I've learned...that everyone wants to live on top of the mountain but all the happiness and growth occurs while you're climbing it.

I've learned...that it is best to give advice in only two circumstances; when it is requested and when it is a life threatening situation.

I've learned...that the less time I have to work, the more things I get done.

Vinton & Michele Stanfield

Military Tradition Continues

John 3:16

A little boy was selling newspapers on the corner as the people were in and out of the cold. He was so cold that he wasn't trying to sell many papers. He walked up to a policeman and said, "Mister, you wouldn't happen to know where a poor boy could find a warm place to sleep tonight would you? You see, I sleep in a box up around the corner there and down the alley and it's awful cold in there for tonight. Sure would be nice to have a warm place to stay."

The policeman looked down at the little boy and said, "You go down the street to that big white house and you knock on the door. When they come out the door you just say 'John 3:16' and they will let you in."

So he did. He walked up the steps, knocked on the door, and a lady answered. He looked up and said, "John 3:16." The lady said, "Come on in, son." She took him in, sat him down in a split bottom rocker in front of a great big old fireplace, and she left. The boy sat there for a while and thought to himself: *John 3:16...I don't understand it, but it sure makes a cold boy warm.*

Later, she came back and asked him "Are you hungry?" He said, "Well, just a little. I haven't eaten in a couple of days and I guess I could stand a little bit of food." The lady took him in the kitchen and sat him down to a table full of wonderful food. He ate and ate until he couldn't eat any more. Then he thought to himself: *John 3:16. Boy, I sure don't understand it but it sure makes a hungry boy full.*

She took him upstairs to a bathroom to a huge bathtub filled with warm water. He sat there and soaked for a while. As he soaked, he thought to himself: *John 3:16. I sure don't understand it but it sure makes a dirty boy clean.* You know, I've not had a bath, a real bath, in my whole life. The only bath I ever had was when I stood in front of that big old fire hydrant as they flushed it out.

The lady came in and got him. She took him to a room, tucked him into a big old feather bed, pulled the covers up around his neck, kissed him goodnight and turned out the lights. As he lay in the darkness and looked out the window at the snow coming down on that cold night, he thought to himself: *John 3:16. I don't understand it but it sure makes a tired boy rested.*

The next morning the lady came and took him down again to that same big table full of food. After he ate, she took him back to that same big old split bottom rocker in front of the fireplace and picked up a big old Bible. She sat down in front of him and looked into his young face. "Do you understand John 3:16?" she asked gently. He replied, "No, Ma'am, I don't. The first time I ever heard it was last night when the policeman told me to use it." She opened the Bible to John 3:16 and began to explain to him about Jesus. Right there, in front of that big old fireplace, he gave his heart and life to Jesus. He sat there and thought: *John 3:16 I don't understand it but it sure makes a lost boy feel safe.*

You know, I have to confess I don't understand it either, how God was willing to send His Son to die for me and how Jesus would agree to do such a thing. I don't understand the agony of the Father and every angel in heaven as they watched Jesus suffer and die. I don't understand the intense love for ME that kept Jesus on the Cross until the end. I don't understand it but it sure does make life worth living.

John 3:16 For God so loved the world, that he gave his only begotten Son, that whosoever believeth in him should not perish, but have everlasting life.

Vinton & Michele Stanfield

Men! Men! Men!

Keeper

I grew up in the 1940's and 50's with practical parents. A mother, God love her, who washed aluminum foil after she cooked in it, then reused it. She was the original recycle queen before they had a name for it. A father who was happier getting old shoes fixed than buying new ones.

Their marriage was good and their dreams focused. Their best friends lived barely a wave away. I can see them now, Dad in trousers, tee shirt and a hat and Mom in a house dress, lawn mower in one hand, and dish-towel in the other. It was the time for fixing things. A curtain rod, the kitchen radio, screen door, the oven door, the hem in a dress...things we keep.

It was a way of life and sometimes it made me crazy with all that re-fixing and renewing. I wanted just once to be wasteful. Waste meant affluence. Throwing things away meant you knew there'd always be more.

But then my mother died and on that clear summer's night, in the warmth of the hospital room, I was struck with the pain of learning that sometimes there isn't any more.

Sometimes, what we care about most gets all used up and goes away...never to return. So while we have it... it's best we love it...and care for it...and fix it when it's broken...and heal it when it's sick.

This is true for marriage...and old cars...and children with bad report cards...and dogs with bad hips...and aging parents...and grandparents. We keep them because they are worth it and because we are worth it. Some things we keep like a best friend that moved away or a classmate we grew up with early in life.

There are just some things that make life important, like people we know who are special and so, we keep them close!

Kids

3-year-old Reese prayed, "Our Father, Who does art in heaven, Harold is His name. Amen."

A little boy was overheard praying, "Lord, if you can't make me a better boy, don't worry about it. I'm having a real good time like I am."

After the christening of his baby brother in church, Jason sobbed all the way home in the back seat of the car. His father asked him three times what was wrong. Finally, the boy replied, "That preacher said he wanted us brought up in a Christian home and I wanted to stay with you guys."

One particular four-year-old prayed, "And forgive us our trash baskets as we forgive those who put trash in our baskets."

A Sunday school teacher asked her children as they were on the way to church service, "And why is it necessary to be quiet in church?" One bright little girl replied, "Because people are sleeping."

A mother was preparing pancakes for her sons, Kevin 5, and Ryan 3. The boys began to argue over who would get the first pancake. Their mother saw the opportunity for a moral lesson. If Jesus was sitting here, she said, He would say, "Let my brother have the first pancake, I can wait." Kevin turned to his younger brother and said, "Ryan, you be Jesus!"

A father was at the beach with his children when the four-year-old son ran up to him, grabbed his hand, and led him to the shore where a seagull lay dead in the sand. "Daddy, what happened to him?" the boy asked. "He died and went to Heaven," the Dad replied. The boy thought a moment and then said, "Did God throw him back down?"

A lady invited a family to dinner. At the table, she turned to their six-year-old daughter and said, "Would you like to say the blessing?" "I wouldn't know what to say," the girl replied. "Just say what you hear your Mommy say," the lady answered. The daughter bowed her head and said, "Lord, why on earth did I invite all these people to dinner?"

Peace, Love and Happiness

Lessons I Learned About Life
(While Working in My Dad's Woodshop)

1. The job is "much more easier" if you have the right tools.

2. Love is like glue; the more you spread it around, the better things stick together.

3. The mark of a great craftsman is not how well you build but how well you hide your mistakes.

4. Never settle for less than your best no matter how great someone thinks your second best is.

5. Give someone else a chance to be creative, who knows, you might learn something.

6. Respect your tools! Pieces of wood are easy to glue back together, whereas body parts are not.

7. Marriage, at times, is like a piece of unfinished wood. You need to work at it until you get the warps out.

8. You can NEVER have too many clamps.

9. "Rustic Quality" is the nice name we give to our mistakes.

10. A bad day in the woodshop is still preferable to a great day at '*work*' (that dirty four letter word!).

Victoria L. Panther

Vinton & Michele Stanfield

In My Dad's Woodshop

Life Under the Moonlight

Where the colorful shapes of heavenly spheres fly
Where a diamond and crystals hang in the night
Shades of black and blue darken the sky.

The owl lifts its wings and soars into flight
While on the ground timid animals feed
Ever fearful of entering a predator's sight.

Light pierces midnight's veil at unimaginable speed
Bursting into millions of facets that gleam
More beautiful than gems that prompt men's greed.

Starry hosts reflect upon a quietly running stream
As silver fish swim in its sparkling glass haze
Tranquilly living in our God's captivating dream.

Suddenly the night is gone with the sun's first blaze
Snuffing out the candles of the stars and moon
And leaving in their wake a gold and sunny glaze.

Brianna Michele Shaver

Vinton & Michele Stanfield

Enjoying Our National Parks

Let's Run Through the Rain

She must have been six years old, this beautiful brown haired, freckled-faced image of innocence. Her mother looked like someone from the Walton's or a moment captured by Norman Rockwell. Not that she was old-fashioned. Her brown hair was ear length with enough curl to appear natural. She had on a pair of tan shorts and light blue knit shirt. Her sneakers were white with a blue trim. She looked like a Mom.

It was pouring outside. The kind of rain that gushes over the tops of rain gutters, so much in a hurry to hit the earth that it has no time to flow down the spout. Drains in the nearby parking lot were filled to capacity and some were blocked so that huge puddles, like lakes, were around parked cars. We all stood there under the awning and just inside the door of the store. We waited, some patiently, others aggravated because nature messed up their hurried day. I am always mesmerized by rainfall. I get lost in the sound and sight of the heavens washing away the dirt and dust of the world. Memories of running, splashing, so carefree as a child come pouring in as a welcome reprieve from the worries of my day.

Her voice was so sweet as it broke the hypnotic trance we were all caught in. "Mom, let's run through the rain," she said. "What?" her mother asked. "Let's run through the rain!" she repeated. "No, honey, we'll wait until it slows down a bit," she replied. This young child waited about another minute and repeated her statement. "Mom, let's run through the rain." "We'll get soaked if we do," Mom said. "No we won't, Mom. That's not what you said this morning," the young girl said as she tugged at her mom's arm. "This morning? When did I say we could run through the rain and not get wet?" "Don't you remember? When you were talking to Daddy about his cancer?" You said, "If God can get us through this, He can get us through anything!"

The entire crowd stopped dead silent. I swear you couldn't hear anything but the rain. We all stood silently. No one came or left in the next few minutes. Mom paused and thought for a moment about what she would say. Now some would laugh it off and scold her for being silly. Some might even ignore what was said. This was a moment of affirmation in a young child's life, a time when innocent trust can be nurtured so that it will bloom into faith. "Honey, you are absolutely right. Let's run through the rain. If God lets us get wet, well maybe we just needed washing," Mom said. Then off they ran.

We all stood watching, smiling and laughing as they darted past the cars and yes, through the puddles. They held their shopping bags over their heads just in case. They got soaked. They were followed by a few believers who screamed and laughed like children all the way to their cars, perhaps inspired by their faith and trust. I want to believe that somewhere down the road in life, Mom will find herself reflecting back on moments they spent together, captured like pictures in the scrapbook of her cherished memories. Maybe, when she watches proudly as her daughter graduates, or as her daddy walks her down the aisle on her wedding day, she will laugh again. Her heart will beat a little faster. Her smile will tell the world they love each other.

Yet only two people will share that precious moment when they ran through the rain believing that God would get them through. And yes, I did. I ran. I got wet. I needed washing.

I HOPE YOU ALL STILL 'HAVE IT IN YOU'...TO RUN THROUGH THE RAIN.

"Amen, I say unto you, whoever does not receive the kingdom of God like a child will not enter therein." - Luke 18:17

Idaho Cowboy

Lord's Baseball Game

Because baseball and home runs are the hot topic these days....Here is a story about the Lord's baseball game.

Bob was caught up in the spirit where he and the Lord stood by to observe a baseball game. The Lord's team was playing Satan's team. The Lord's team was at bat. The score was tied zero to zero and it was the bottom of the ninth inning with two outs. They continued to watch as a batter stepped up to the plate whose name was Love. Love swung at the first pitch and hit a single because Love never fails. The next batter was named Faith, who also got a single because Faith works with Love. The next batter was named Godly Wisdom. Satan wound up and threw the first pitch. Godly Wisdom looked it over and let it pass because Godly Wisdom does not swing at Satan's pitches. Ball one. Three more pitches and Godly Wisdom walked because Godly Wisdom never swings at what Satan throws. The bases were loaded. The Lord then turned to Bob and told him He was now going to bring in His star player. Up to the plate stepped Grace. Thinking he had won the game, Satan wound up and fired his first pitch. To the shock of everyone, Grace hit the ball harder than anyone had ever seen but Satan was not worried. His center fielder, the Prince of the air, let very few get by him. He went up for the ball but it went right through his glove, hit him on the head, sent him crashing on the ground and then it continued over the fence for a home run! The Lord's team won.

The Lord then asked Bob if he knew why Love, Faith, and Godly Wisdom could get on base but could not win the game. Bob answered that he did not know why. The Lord explained, "If your love, faith and wisdom had won the game you would think you had done it by yourself. Love, Faith and Wisdom will get you on base but only My Grace can get you home because it is the one thing Satan cannot stop!"

Meet ME in the Stair Well!

You say you will never forget where you were when you heard the news on September 11, 2001…neither will I.

I was on the 110th floor in a smoke filled room with a man who called his wife to say "Good-Bye." I held his fingers steady as he dialed. I gave him the peace to say, "Honey, I am not going to make it, but it is OK. I am ready to go."

I was with his wife when he called as she fed breakfast to their children. I held her up as she tried to understand his words and as she realized he wasn't coming home that night.

I was in the stairwell of the 23rd floor when a woman cried out to Me for help. "I have been knocking on the door of your heart for 50 years!" I said. "Of course I will show you the way home – only believe in Me now."

I was at the base of the building with the Priest ministering to the injured and devastated souls. I took him home to tend to his flock in Heaven. He heard my voice and answered.

I was on all four of those planes, in every seat, with every prayer. I was with the crew as they were overtaken. I was in the very hearts of the believers there, comforting and assuring them that their faith has saved them.

I was in Texas, Virginia, California, Michigan, and Afghanistan. I was standing next to you when you heard the terrible news. Did you sense Me?

I want you to know that I saw every face. I knew every name - though not all knew Me. Some met Me for the first time on the 86th floor.

Some sought Me with their last breath. Some couldn't hear Me calling to them through the smoke and flames; "Come to Me... this way... take my hand." Some chose, for the final time, to ignore Me but I was there.

I did not place you in the Tower that day. You may not know why, but I do. However, if you were there in that explosive moment in time, would you have reached for Me?

September 11, 2001, was not the end of the journey for you. But someday your journey will end. And I will be there for you as well. Seek Me, now, while I may be found. Then, at any moment, you know you are 'ready to go'.

I will be in the stairwell of your final moments...God

Remember Your ABC'S
TO ACHIEVE YOUR GOALS

Avoid negative sources, people, places, things, and habits.

Believe in yourself.

Consider things from every angle.

Don't give up and don't give in.

Enjoy life; yesterday is gone; tomorrow may never come.

Family and friends are hidden treasures; seek them and enjoy their riches.

Give more than you planned.

Hang on to your dreams.

Ignore those who try to discourage you.

Just do it!

Keep trying no matter how hard it seems; it will get easier.

Love yourself first and foremost.

Make it happen.

Never lie, cheat, or steal; always strike a fair deal.

Open your eyes and see things as they really are.

Practice makes perfect.

Quitters never win and winners never quit.

Read, study and learn about everything important in your life.

Stop procrastinating.

Take control of your own destiny.

Understand yourself in order to better understand others.

Visualize it.

Want it more than anything.

Xcelerate your efforts.

You are unique among all of God's creations.

Zero in on your target and go for it!

Fantastic and Getting Better!

Seems Almost Too Much To Handle

When things in your life seem almost too much to handle, when twenty-four hours in a day are not enough, remember the mayonnaise jar and the two glasses of wine...

A professor stood before his philosophy class and had some items in front of him. When the class began, wordlessly, he picked up a very large and empty mayonnaise jar and proceeded to fill it with golf balls. He then asked the students if the jar was full. They agreed that it was. The professor then picked up a box of pebbles and poured them into the jar. He shook the jar lightly. The pebbles rolled into the open areas between the golf balls. He then asked the students again if the jar was full. They agreed it was.

The professor next picked up a box of sand and poured it into the jar. Of course, the sand filled up everything else. He asked once more if the jar was full. The students responded with a unanimous "yes." The professor then produced two glasses of wine from under the table and poured the entire contents into the jar, effectively filling the empty space between the sand. The students laughed.

"Now," said the professor, as the laughter subsided, "I want you to recognize that this jar represents your life. The golf balls are the important things -- your God, your family, your children, your health, your friends, and your favorite passions -- things that if everything else was lost and only they remained, your life would still be full. The pebbles are the other things that matter like your job, your house, and your car. The sand is everything else -- the small stuff. If you put the sand into the jar first," he continued, "there is no room for the pebbles or the golf balls. The same goes for life. If you spend all your time and energy on the small stuff, you will never have room for the things that are important to you. Pay attention to the things that are critical to your happiness. Play with your children. Take time to get medical checkups. Take your spouse out to dinner. Play another 18. There will always be time to clean the house and fix the disposal. Take care of the golf balls first -- the things that really matter. Set your priorities. The rest is just sand."

One of the students raised her hand and inquired what the wine represented. The professor smiled. "I'm glad you asked. It just goes to show you that no matter how full your life may seem, there's always room for a couple of glasses of wine with a friend."

Senior Wedding

Jacob, age 92, and Rebecca, age 89, living in Miami, were all excited about their decision to get married. They went for a stroll to discuss the wedding. While walking they passed a drugstore and Jacob suggested they go inside.

Jacob addressed the man behind the counter. "Are you the owner?"

The pharmacist answered, "Yes, sir."

Jacob: "We're about to get married. Do you sell heart medication?"

Pharmacist: "Of course, we do."

Jacob: "How about medicine for circulation?"

Pharmacist: "All kinds."

Jacob: "Medicine for rheumatism?"

Pharmacist: "Definitely."

Jacob: "How about suppositories?"

Pharmacist: "You bet!"

Jacob: "Medicine for memory problems, arthritis and Alzheimer's?"

Pharmacist: "Yes, a large variety. The works!"

Jacob: "What about vitamins, sleeping pills, Geritol, and antidotes for Parkinson's disease?"

Pharmacist: "Absolutely."

Jacob: "Everything for heartburn and indigestion?"

Pharmacist: "We sure do."

Jacob: "You sell wheelchairs and walkers and canes?"

Pharmacist: "All speeds and sizes."

Jacob: "Adult diapers?"

Pharmacist: "Sure."

Jacob: "Great! We would like to use this store as our Bridal Registry."

Seven Advices of Mevlâna

>1<
In generosity and helping others,
be like a river.

>2<
In compassion and grace,
be like the sun.

>3<
In concealing others' faults,
be like the night.

>4<
In anger and fury,
be like the dead.

>5<
In modesty and humility,
be like the earth,

>6<
In tolerance,
be like the sea.

>7<
Either exist as you are,
or be as you look.

Ismet Keten

Vinton & Michele Stanfield

Our "Harika" Turkish Family

The Sack Lunch

I put my carry-on in the luggage compartment and sat down in my assigned seat. It was going to be a long flight. *"I'm glad I have a good book to read. Perhaps I will get a short nap,"* I thought.

Just before take-off, a line of soldiers came down the aisle and filled all the vacant seats, totally surrounding me. I decided to start a conversation. "Where are you headed?" I asked the soldier seated next to me. He replied, "Chicago, and then on to Great Lakes Base. We'll be there for two weeks for Special training, and then we're being deployed to Iraq."

After flying for about an hour, an announcement was made that sack lunches were available for five dollars. It would be several hours before we reached Chicago and I quickly decided a lunch would help pass the time. As I reached for my wallet, I overheard a soldier ask his buddy if he had planned to buy lunch. "No, that seems like a lot of money for just a sack lunch. Probably wouldn't be worth five bucks. I'll wait till we get to Chicago." His friend agreed.

I looked around at the other soldiers. None were buying lunch. I walked to the back of the plane and handed the flight attendant a fifty dollar bill. "Take a lunch to all those soldiers." She grabbed my arms and squeezed tightly. Her eyes filled with tears, she thanked me. "My son is a soldier in Iraq; it's almost like you are doing it for him."

Picking up ten sacks, she headed up the aisle to where the soldiers were seated. She stopped at my seat and asked, "Which do you like best - beef or chicken?" "Chicken," I replied, wondering why she asked. She turned and went to the front of plane, returning a minute later with a dinner plate from first class. "This is your and thanks." After we finished eating, I went again to the back of the plane, heading for the rest room. A man stopped me. "I saw what you did. I want to be part of your efforts. Here, take this." He handed me twenty-five dollars.

Soon after I returned to my seat, I saw the Flight Captain coming down the aisle looking at the aisle numbers as he walked. I hoped he was not looking for me but noticed he was looking at the numbers only on my side of the plane. When he got to my row he stopped, smiled, held out his hand, and said, "I want to shake your hand." Quickly unfastening my seatbelt I stood and took the Captain's hand. With a booming voice he said, "I was a soldier and I was a military pilot. Once, someone bought me a lunch. It was an act of kindness I never forgot." I was embarrassed when applause was heard from all of the passengers. Later I walked to the front of the plane so I could stretch my legs. A man who was seated about six rows in front of me reached out his hand, wanting to shake mine. He left another twenty-five dollars in my palm.

When we landed in Chicago I gathered my belongings and started to deplane. Waiting just inside the airplane door was a man who stopped me, put something in my shirt pocket, turned, and walked away without saying a word. Another twenty-five dollars!

Soon entering the terminal, I saw the soldiers gathering for their trip to the base. I walked over to them and handed them seventy-five dollars. "It will take you some time to reach the base. It will be about time for a sandwich. God Bless You."

Ten young men left that flight feeling the love and respect of their fellow travelers. As I walked briskly to my car, I whispered a prayer for their safe return. These soldiers were giving their all for our country. I could only give them a couple of meals. It seemed so little.

A veteran is someone who, at one point in their life wrote a blank check made payable to "The United States of America" for an amount of "up to and including their life." That is honor, and there are way too many people in this country who no longer understand it.

Vinton & Michele Stanfield

Young and old remembering our Service Members

The Wooden Bowl

A frail old man went to live with his son, daughter-in-law, and four-year grandson. The old man's hands trembled, his eyesight was blurred, and his step faltered. The family ate together at the table but the elderly grandfather's shaky hands and failing sight made eating difficult. Peas rolled off his spoon onto the floor. When he grasped the glass, milk spilled on the tablecloth.

The son and daughter-in-law became irritated with the mess. "We must do something about Grandfather," said the son. "I've had enough of his spilled milk, noisy eating, and food on the floor." So the husband and wife set a small table in the corner. There, Grandfather ate alone while the rest of the family enjoyed their meals at the table. Since Grandfather had broken a dish or two, his food was served in a wooden bowl. When the family glanced in his direction, sometimes he had a tear in his eye as he sat alone. Still, the only words the couple had for him were sharp admonitions when he dropped a fork or spilled food.

The four-year-old watched it all in silence. One evening before supper, the father noticed his son playing with wood scraps on the floor. He asked the child sweetly, "What are you making?" Just as sweetly, the boy responded, "Oh, I am making a little bowl for you and Mama to eat your food when I grow up." The four-year-old smiled and went back to work. The words so struck the parents that they were speechless. Then tears started to stream down their cheeks. Though no word was spoken, both knew what must be done. That evening the husband took Grandfather's hand and gently led him back to the family table. For the remainder of his days he ate every meal with the family and for some reason neither, husband nor wife, seemed to care any longer when a fork was dropped, milk spilled, or the tablecloth soiled.

* * *

I've learned that no matter what happens or how bad it seems today, life does go on, and it will be better tomorrow.

I've learned that you can tell a lot about a person by the way he/she handles three things: a rainy day, lost luggage, and tangled Christmas tree lights.

I've learned that, regardless of your relationship with your parents, you'll miss them when they're gone from your life.

I've learned that making a 'living' is not the same thing as making a 'life' and that life sometimes gives you a second chance.

I've learned that you shouldn't go through life with a catcher's mitt on both hands. You need to be able to throw something back.

I've learned that if you pursue happiness, it will elude you. If you focus on your family, your friends, the needs of others, your work and doing the very best you can, happiness will find you.

I've learned that whenever I decide something with an open heart, I usually make the right decision.

I've learned that even when I have pain, I don't have to be one.

I've learned that every day, you should reach out and touch someone. People love that human touch of holding hands, a warm hug, or just a friendly pat on the back.

I've learned that I still have a lot to learn.

I've learned that people will forget what you said, will forget what you did, but will never forget how you made them feel.

Vinton & Michele Stanfield

So Many to Remember from 9/11

Three Trees

Once there were three trees on a hill in the woods. They were discussing their hopes and dreams when the first tree said, "Someday I hope to be a treasure chest. I could be filled with gold, silver and precious gems. I could be decorated with intricate carving and everyone would see the beauty."

Then the second tree said, "Someday I will be a mighty ship. I will take kings and queens across the waters and sail to all the corners of the world. Everyone will feel safe in me because of the strength of my hull."

Finally, the third tree said, "I want to grow to be the tallest and straightest tree in the forest. People will see me on top of the hill. They will look up to my branches and think of the heavens, of God and how close to them I am reaching. I will be the greatest tree of all time and people will always remember me."

After a few years of praying that their dreams would come true, a group of woodsmen came upon the trees. When one came to the first tree he said, "This looks like a strong tree, I think I should be able to sell the wood to a carpenter" and he began cutting it down. The tree was happy because he knew that the carpenter would make him into a treasure chest.

At the second tree a woodsman said, "This looks like a strong tree and I should be able to sell it to the shipyard." The second tree was happy because he knew he was on his way to becoming a mighty ship.

When the woodsmen came upon the third tree, the tree was frightened because he just knew that if they cut him down his dreams would not come true. One of the woodsmen said, "I don't need anything special from my tree so I'll take this one" and he cut it down.

When the first tree arrived at the carpenter's, he was made into a feed box for animals. He was then placed in a barn and filled with hay. This was not at all what he had wanted. The second tree was cut and made into a small fishing boat. His dreams of being a mighty ship and carrying kings had come to an end also. The third tree was cut into large pieces and left alone in the dark. The years went by and the trees forgot about their dreams.

Then one day a man and woman came to the barn. She gave birth and they placed the baby in the hay in the feed box that was made from the first tree. The man wished that he could have made a crib for the baby but this manger would have to suffice. The tree could feel the importance of this event and knew that it had held the greatest treasure of all time.

Years later, a group of men got in the fishing boat made from the second tree. One of them was tired and went to sleep. While they were out on the water a great storm arose and the tree didn't think it was strong enough to keep the men safe. The men woke the sleeping man. He stood and said "Peace" and the storm stopped. At this time, the tree knew that it had carried the King of Kings in its boat.

Finally, someone came and got the third tree. It was

carried through the streets as the people mocked the man who was carrying it. When they came to a hill, the man was nailed to the tree and raised in the air to die. He was brought down and buried. When Sunday came, the tree came to realize that it was strong enough to stand at the top of the hill and be as close to God as was possible because Jesus had been crucified on it.

The moral of this story is that when things don't seem to be going your way, always know that God has a plan for you. If you place your trust in Him, He will give you great gifts. Each of the trees got what they wanted just not in the way they had imagined. We don't always know what God's plans are for us. We just know that His ways are not our ways but **His ways are always best.**

With Friends in Turkey

Fantastic and Getting Better!

To All the Kids Who Survived
the 1930's 40's, 50's, 60's and 70's!

We survived being born to mothers who smoked and/or drank while they carried us.

They took aspirin, ate blue cheese dressing, tuna from a can, and didn't get tested for diabetes.

Our baby cribs were covered with bright colored lead-based paints.

We had no child proof lids on medicine bottles, doors or cabinets and when we rode our bikes, we had no helmets, not to mention, the risks we took hitchhiking.

As children, we would ride in cars with no seat belts or air bags. Riding in the back of a pick-up on a warm day was always a special treat.

We drank water from the garden hose and not from a bottle.

We shared one soft drink with four friends, from one bottle and no one actually died from this.

We ate cupcakes, white bread, real butter and drank soda pop with sugar in it but we weren't overweight because…we were always outside…playing! We would leave home in the morning and play all day, as long as we were back when the streetlights came on. No one was able to reach us all day and we were OK.

We would spend hours building our go-carts out of scraps and then ride down the hill, only to find out we forgot the brakes. After running into the bushes a few times, we learned to solve the problem.

We did not have Play-stations, Nintendo's, X-boxes, no video games at all, no ninety-plus channels on cable (actual no cable TV), no video tape movies, no surround sound, no cell phones, no personal computers, no Internet or Internet chat rooms. We had friends…and we went outside and found them!

We fell out of trees, got cut, broke bones and teeth and there were no lawsuits from these accidents.

We ate worms and mud pies made from dirt and the worms did not live in us forever.

We were given BB guns for our 10th birthdays, made up games with sticks and tennis balls and although we were told it would happen, we did not put out very many eyes.

We rode bikes or walked to a friend's house and knocked on the door or rang the bell, or just walked in and talked to them!

Little League had tryouts and not everyone made the team. Those who didn't had to learn to deal with disappointment. Imagine that!

The idea of a parent bailing us out if we broke the law was unheard of where we lived. They actually sided with the law!

This generation has produced some of the best risk-takers, problem solvers and inventors ever!

The past 50 years have been an explosion of innovation and new ideas. We had freedom, failure, success and responsibility…and we learned how to deal with it all!

And if YOU are one of Us… CONGRATULATIONS!

Vinton & Michele Stanfield

Best Friends Forever

T'was the Night Before Christmas

He lived all alone,
in a one bedroom house made of plaster and stone.

I had come down the chimney with presents to give,
and to see just who, in this home, did live.

I looked all about a strange sight I did see,
no tinsel, no presents, not even a tree.

No stocking by the mantle, just boots filled with sand,
on the wall hung pictures of a far distant land.

With medals and badges, awards of all kinds,
a sobering thought came through my mind.

For this house was different, it was dark and dreary.
I had found the home of some soldier, once I could see clearly.

He lay sleeping, silent, alone,
curled-up on the floor in this one bedroom home.

The face was so gentle, the room in such disorder,
not how I pictured a United States soldier.

Was this the hero of whom I'd just read,
curled up on a poncho, the floor for a bed?

I realized the families that I saw this night,
owed their lives to these soldiers who were willing to fight.

Soon round the world the children would play,
and grownups would celebrate a bright Christmas day.

They all enjoyed freedom each month of the year,
because of the soldiers, like the one lying here.

I couldn't help wonder how many lay alone,
on a cold Christmas eve in a land far from home.

The very thought brought a tear to my eye.
I dropped to my knees and started to cry.

The soldier awakened and I heard a rough voice,
"Santa, don't cry, my life is my choice.

I fight for freedom, I don't ask for more.
My life is my God, my Country, my Corps."

The soldier rolled over and drifted to sleep,
I couldn't control it, I continued to weep.

I kept watch for hours, so silent and still,
We both were shivering from the cold night's chill.

I didn't want to leave on that cold, dark night,
this guardian of honor so willing to fight.

Then the soldier rolled over, with a voice soft and pure, whispered, "Carry on Santa, it's Christmas day, all is secure."

One look at my watch, and I knew he was right, "Merry Christmas, my friend, and to all a good night."

This poem was written by a marine stationed in Okinawa, Japan.

Veterans Day in Liberty Hill, Texas

Unfolding the Rosebud

A young, new preacher was walking with an older, more seasoned preacher in the garden one day. Feeling a bit insecure about what God had for him to do, he was inquiring of the older man. The older preacher walked up to a rosebush and handed the young man a rosebud and told him to open it without tearing off any petals. The young preacher looked in disbelief at the older one and was trying to figure out what a rosebud could possibly have to do with his wanting to know the will of God for his life and for his ministry.

Because of his high respect for the older preacher, he proceeded to try to unfold the rose, while keeping every petal intact. It wasn't long before he realized how impossible it was to do.

Noticing the younger preacher's inability to unfold the rosebud while keeping it in tact, the older preacher recited the following poem:

"UNFOLDING THE ROSEBUD"

It is only a tiny rosebud,
A flower of God's design.
I cannot unfold the petals,
With these clumsy hands of mine.

The secret of unfolding flowers,
Is not known to such as I.
God opens the flower so sweetly,
When in my hands they fade and die.

If I cannot unfold a rosebud,
This flower of God's design.
Then how can I think I have wisdom,
To unfold this life of mine?

I'll have to trust in Him for His leading,
Each moment of every day.
I will look to Him for guidance,
Each step of the pilgrim's way.

The pathway that lies before me,
Only my heavenly Father knows.
I'll trust Him to unfold the moments,
Just as He unfolds the rose.

Fantastic and Getting Better!

What Does Love Mean?
Touching Words From the Little People

A group of professional people posed this question to a group of four to eight year olds , "What does love mean?" The answers they received were broader and deeper than anyone could have imagined.

"When my grandmother got arthritis, she couldn't bend over and paint her toenails anymore. So my grandfather does it for her all the time, even when his hands got arthritis too. That's love."   Rebecca- age 8

"When someone loves you, the way they say your name is different. You just know that your name is safe in their mouth."   Billy - age 4

"Love is when a girl puts on perfume and a boy puts on shaving cologne and they go out and smell each other." Karl - age 5

"Love is when you go out to eat and give somebody most of your french-fries without making them give you any of theirs."   Christy - age 6

"Love is what makes you smile when you're tired." Terri - age 4

"Love is when my mommy makes coffee for my daddy and she takes a sip before giving it to him, to make sure the taste is OK." Danny - age 7

~ 183 ~

"Love is when you kiss all the time. Then when you get tired of kissing, you still want to be together and you talk more. My mommy and daddy are like that. They look gross when they kiss."   Emily - age 8

"Love is what's in the room with you at Christmas if you stop opening presents and listen."   Bobby - age 7

"If you want to learn to love better, you should start with a friend who you hate."   Nikka - age 6

"Love is when you tell a guy you like his shirt, then, he wears it every day."   Noelle - age 7

"Love is like a little old woman and a little old man who are still friends even after they know each other so well." Tommy - age 6

"During my piano recital, I was on a stage and I was scared. I looked at all the people watching me and saw my daddy waving and smiling. He was the only one doing that. I wasn't scared anymore."   Cindy - age 8

"My mommy loves me more than anybody. You don't see anyone else kissing me to sleep at night."   Clare - age 6

"Love is when Mommy gives Daddy the best piece of chicken."   Elaine-age 5

"Love is when Mommy sees Daddy smelly and sweaty and still says he is handsomer than Robert Redford."
Chris - age 7

"Love is when your puppy licks your face even after you left him alone all day."   Mary Ann - age 4

"I know my older sister loves me because she gives me all her old clothes and has to go out and buy new ones."
Lauren - age 4

"When you love somebody, your eyelashes go up and down and little stars come out of you."   Karen - age 7

"You really shouldn't say 'I love you' unless you mean it. But if you mean it, you should say it a lot. People forget."
Jessica - age 8

A four year old child was watching his next door neighbor, an elderly gentleman who had recently lost his wife. Upon seeing the man cry, the little boy went into the old gentleman's yard, climbed onto his lap, and just sat there. When his mother asked what he had said to the neighbor, the little boy said, "Nothing, I just helped him cry."

Thank you, God, for all the children in this world…no matter where they live, no matter their ethnicity, no matter their social standing, no matter. Love is love.

Vinton & Michele Stanfield

'Blue-water' Canadian Best Friends

What God Can Do With Fifty-Seven Cents

During the early 1900's, a sobbing little girl stood near a small church from which she had been turned away because it was too crowded.

"I can't go to Sunday School," she sobbed to the pastor as he walked by. Seeing her shabby, unkempt appearance, the pastor guessed the reason and, taking her by the hand, took her inside and found a place for her in the Sunday school class. The child was so touched that she went to bed that night thinking of the children who have no place to worship.

Some two years later, this same child lay dead in one of the poor tenement buildings and the parents called for the kind-hearted pastor, who had befriended their daughter, to handle the final arrangements. As her poor little body was being moved, a worn and crumpled purse was found which seemed to have been rummaged from some trash dump. Inside was found fifty-seven cents and a note scribbled in childish handwriting which read, "This is to help build the little church bigger so more children can go to Sunday school." For two years she had saved for this offering of love. When the pastor tearfully read that note, he knew instantly what he would do.

Carrying this note and the cracked, red purse to the pulpit, he told the story of her unselfish love and devotion. He challenged his deacons to get busy and raise enough money for the larger building.

But the story does not end there! A newspaper learned of the story and published it. It was read by a realtor who offered them a parcel of land worth many thousands. When told that the church could not pay so much, he offered it for the fifty-seven cents. Church members made large subscriptions.

Checks came from far and wide. Within five years the little girl's gift had increased to a quarter of a million dollars. Her unselfish love had paid large dividends.

When you are in the city of Philadelphia, look up Temple Baptist Church, with a seating capacity of several thousand, and Temple University, where hundreds of students are trained. Have a look, too, at the Good Samaritan Hospital and at a Sunday school building which houses hundreds of Sunday scholars, so that no child in the area will ever need to be left outside during Sunday school time. In one of the rooms of this building may be seen the picture of the sweet face of the little girl whose fifty-seven cents, so sacrificially saved, made such remarkable history.

Alongside of it, is a portrait of her kind pastor, Dr. Russell H. Conwell, author of the book, "Acres of Diamonds" - a true story.

Goes to show what GOD can do with fifty-seven cents.

What I Have Learned in Life!

Age 6…I've learned that I like my teacher because she cries when we sing "Silent Night".
Age 7…I've learned that our dog doesn't want to eat my broccoli either.
Age 8…I've learned that when I wave to people in the country, they stop what they are doing and wave back.
Age 9…I've learned that just when I get my room the way I like it, Mom makes me clean it up again.
Age 12..I've learned that if you want to cheer yourself up, you should try cheering someone else up.
Age 14..I've learned that although it's hard to admit it, I'm secretly glad my parents are strict with me.
Age 15..I've learned that silent company is often more healing than words of advice.
Age 24..I've learned that brushing my child's hair is one of life's great pleasures.
Age 26..I've learned that wherever I go, the world's worst drivers have followed me there.
Age 29..I've learned that if someone says something unkind about me, I must live so that no one will believe it.
Age 39..I've learned that there are people who love you dearly but just don't know how to show it.
Age 42..I've learned that you can make someone's day by simply sending them a little note.
Age 44.. I've learned that the greater a person's sense of guilt, the greater his or her need to cast blame on others.
Age 46..I've learned that children and grandparents are natural allies.

Age 47..I've learned that no matter what happens or how bad it seems today, life does go on, and it will be better tomorrow.

Age 48..I've learned that singing "Amazing Grace" can lift my spirits for hours.

Age 49..I've learned that motel mattresses are better on the side away from the phone.

Age 50..I've learned that you can tell a lot about a man by the way he handles these three things: a rainy day, lost luggage, and tangled Christmas tree lights.

Age 51..I've learned that keeping a vegetable garden is worth a medicine cabinet full of pills.

Age 52..I've learned that regardless of your relationship with your parents, you miss them terribly after they die.

Age 53..I've learned that making a living is not the same thing as making a life.

Age 58..I've learned that if you want to do something positive for your children, work to improve your marriage.

Age 61..I've learned that life sometimes gives you a second chance.

Age 62..I've learned that you shouldn't go through life with a catcher's mitt on both hands. You need to be able to throw something back.

Age 64..I've learned that if you pursue happiness, it will elude you. Instead, if you focus on your family, the needs of others, your work, meeting new people, and doing the very best you can, happiness will find you.

Age 65..I've learned that whenever I decide something with kindness, I usually make the right decision.

Age 66..I've learned that everyone can use a prayer.
Age 72..I've learned that it pays to believe in miracles and to tell the truth I've seen several.
Age 75..I've learned that even when I have pain, I don't have to be one.
Age 82..I've learned that every day you should reach out and touch someone. People love that human touch – holding hands, a warm hug, or just a friendly pat on the back.
Age 92..I've learned that I still have a lot to learn.

Six Generations Ago

What If...?

What if GOD couldn't take the time to bless us today because we couldn't take the time to thank Him yesterday?

What if GOD decided to stop leading us tomorrow because we didn't follow Him today?

What if we never saw another flower bloom because we grumbled when GOD sent the rain?

What if GOD didn't walk with us today because we failed to recognize it as His day?

What if GOD took away the Bible tomorrow because we would not read it today?

What if GOD took away His message because we failed to listen to the messenger?

What if GOD didn't send His only begotten Son because He wanted us to be prepared to pay the price for sin?

What if the door of the church was closed because we did not open the door of our heart?

What if GOD stopped loving and caring for us because we failed to love and care for others?

What if GOD would not hear us today because we would not listen to Him yesterday?

What if GOD answered our prayers the way we answer His call to service?

What if GOD met our needs the way we give Him our lives?

What Is Crucifixion?

A medical doctor provides a physical description:

The cross is placed on the ground and the exhausted man is quickly thrown backwards with his shoulders against the wood.

The legionnaire feels for the depression at the front of the wrist. He drives a heavy, square wrought iron nail through the wrist deep into the wood. Quickly he moves to the other side and repeats the action, being careful not to pull the arms too tightly but to allow some flex and movement.

The cross is then lifted into place. The left foot is pressed backward against the right foot and with both feet extended, toes down, a nail is driven through the arch of each, leaving the knees flexed. The victim is now crucified.

As he slowly sags down with more weight on the nails in the wrists, excruciating fiery pain shoots along the fingers and up the arms to explode in the brain - the nails in the wrists are putting pressure on the median nerves. As he pushes himself upward to avoid this stretching torment, he places the full weight on the nail through his feet. Again he feels the searing agony of the nail tearing through the nerves between the bones of his feet. As the arms fatigue, cramps sweep through his muscles, knotting them a deep relentless and throbbing pain.

With these cramps comes the inability to push himself upward to breathe. Air can be drawn into the lungs but not exhaled. He fights to raise himself in order to get even one small breath. Finally, carbon dioxide builds up in the lungs and in the blood stream, and the cramps partially subside. Spasmodically, he is able to push himself upward to exhale and bring in life-giving oxygen. It may be hours of limitless pain, cycles of twisting, joint wrenching cramps, intermittent partial asphyxiation, searing pain as tissue is torn from his lacerated back as he moves up and down against rough timber.

Then another agony begins: a crushing pain deep in the chest as the pericardium slowly fills with serum and begins to compress the heart. It is now almost over - the loss of tissue fluids has reached a critical level--the compressed heart is struggling to pump heavy, thick, sluggish blood into the tissues--the tortured lungs are making frantic effort to gasp in small gulps of air. He can feel the chill of death creeping through his tissues. Finally, he can allow his body to die.

All this the Bible records with the simple words, *"and they crucified Him" (Mark 15:24).* What wondrous love is this? Many people don't know the pain and suffering our Lord, Jesus Christ experienced for us...because of the brutality, crucifixion was given a sentence to only its worst offenders of the law. Thieves, murderers, and rapists would be the types of people who would be crucified.

Yet here, Jesus is being crucified between two hardened criminals. What did Jesus do? Did he murder anyone? Did he steal anything? The answer as we all know is NO! Jesus did nothing to deserve this type of death, yet he went willing to die, in between two thieves, so that we might be saved. There, in between the sinners, was our slain Savior for our sins.

Brother and Sisters

What My Mother Taught Me

My mother taught me **TO APPRECIATE A JOB WELL DONE**..."If you're going to kill each other, do it outside, I just finished cleaning."

My mother taught me **RELIGION**..."You better pray that will come out of the carpet."

My mother taught me about **TIME TRAVEL**… "If you don't straighten up, I'm going to knock you into the middle of next week!"

My mother taught me **LOGIC**..."Because I said so, that's why."

My mother taught me **FORESIGHT**…"Make sure you wear clean underwear in case you're in an accident."

My mother taught me **IRONY**…"Keep laughing and I'll give you something to cry about."

My mother taught me about the science of **OSMOSIS**… "Shut your mouth and eat your supper!"

My mother taught me about **CONTORTIONISM**… "Will you look at the dirt on the back of your neck?"

My mother taught me about **STAMINA**… "You'll sit there until all that spinach is finished."

My mother taught me about **WEATHER**… "It looks as if a tornado swept through your room."

My mother taught me how to solve **PHYSICS PROBLEMS**… "If I yelled because I saw a meteor coming toward you; would you listen then?"

My mother taught me about **HYPOCRISY**… "If I've told you once, I've told you a million times - Don't exaggerate!"

My mother taught me **THE CIRCLE OF LIFE**… "I brought you into this world and I can take you out."

My mother taught me about **BEHAVIOR MODIFICATION**… "Stop acting like your father!"

My mother taught me about **ENVY**… "There are millions of less fortunate children in this world who don't have wonderful parents like you do!"

THANKS, MOM!

Why Didn't We Have a Drug Problem?

The other day, someone at a store in a small town read that a 'methamphetamine' lab had been found in an old farmhouse in the adjoining county and he asked me a rhetorical question, "Why didn't we have a **drug** problem when you and I were growing up?"

I told him that I did have a **drug** problem when I was a kid growing up on the farm: I was **drug** to church on Sunday morning. I was **drug** to church for weddings and funerals. I was **drug** to family reunions and community socials no matter the weather nor how I was feeling about it.

I was **drug** by my ears when I was disrespectful to adults. I was also **drug** to the woodshed when I disobeyed my parents, told a lie, brought home a bad report card, did not speak with respect, spoke ill of the teacher or the preacher, or if I didn't put forth my best effort in everything that was asked of me.

I was **drug** to the kitchen sink if I uttered a profane four-letter word. (I do know what Lye soap tastes like.)

I was **drug** out to pull weeds in mom's garden and flowerbeds and cockleburs out of dad's fields. I was **drug** to the homes of family, friends, and neighbors to help out some poor soul who had no one, to mow the yard, repair the clothesline or chop some fire wood, and if my mother had ever known that I took a single dime as a tip for this kindness, she would have **drug** me back to the wood shed.

Those **drugs** are still in my veins; and they affect my behavior in everything I do, say, and think. They are stronger than cocaine, crack or heroin, and if today's children had this kind of a **drug** problem, America might be a better place today.

Why GOD Made Moms

Answers given by 2nd grade school children to the following questions:

Why did God make Mothers?
1. She's the only one who knows where the scotch tape is.
2. Mostly to clean the house.
3. To help us out of there when we were getting born.

How did God make Mothers?
1. He used dirt, just like for the rest of us.
2. Magic plus super powers and a lot of stirring.
3. God made my mom just the same like he made me. He just used bigger parts.

From what ingredients are Mothers made?
1. God makes mothers out of clouds and angel hair and everything nice in the world and one dab of mean.
2. They had to get their start from men's bones. Then they mostly use string, I think.

Why did God give you your Mother and not some other Mom?
1. We're related.
2. God knew she likes me a lot more than other people's moms like me.

What kind of little girl was your Mom?
1. My mom has always been my mom and none of that other stuff.

2. I don't know because I wasn't there, but my guess would be pretty bossy.
3. They say she used to be nice.

What did your Mom need to know about your Dad before she married him?
1. His last name.
2. She had to know his background. Like is he a crook? Does he get drunk on beer?
3. Does he make at least $800 a year? Did he say NO to drugs and YES to chores?

Why did your Mom marry your Dad?
1. My dad makes the best spaghetti in the world and my mom eats a lot.
2. She got too old to do anything else with him.
3. My grandma says that mom wasn't using her thinking cap.

Who's the boss at your house?
1. Mom doesn't want to be boss, but she has to because Dad's such a goof ball.
2. Mom. You can tell by room inspection. She sees the stuff under the bed.
3. I guess Mom is but only because she has a lot more to do than Dad.

What's the difference between Mom's & Dad's?
1. Moms work at work and work at home and dads just go to work at work.
2. Moms know how to talk to teachers without scaring them.

3. Dads are taller & stronger, but Moms have all the real power 'cause that's who you got to ask if you want to sleep over at your friend's.

4. Moms have magic; they make you feel better without medicine.

What does your Mom do in her spare time?
1. Mothers don't do spare time.
2. To hear her tell it, she pays bills all day long.

What would it take to make your Mom perfect?
1. On the inside she's already perfect. Outside, I think some kind of plastic surgery.
2. Diet. You know, her hair. I'd diet, maybe blue.

If you could change one thing about your Mom, what would it be?
1. She has this weird thing about me keeping my room clean. I'd get rid of that.
2. I'd make my mom smarter. Then she would know it was my sister who did it and not me.
3. I would like for her to get rid of those invisible eyes on the back of her head.

"Bet you can't do this."

Fantastic and Getting Better!

Why Parents Have Grey Hair!

The boss of a big company needed to call one of his employees about an urgent problem with one of the main computers. He dialed the individual's home phone number and was greeted with a child's whispered, "Hello?" Feeling inconvenienced of having to talk to a youngster, the boss asked, "Is your daddy home?" "Yes," whispered the small voice. "May I talk with him?" the man asked. To the surprise of the boss, the small voice whispered, "No." Wanting to talk with an adult, the boss asked, "Is your mommy there?" "Yes," came the answer. "May I talk with her?" Again the small voice whispered, "No."

Knowing that it was not likely that a young child would be left home alone, the boss decided he would just leave a message with the person who should be there watching over the child. "Is there any one there besides you?" the boss asked the child. "Yes," whispered the child, "a policeman." Wondering what a cop would be doing at his employee's home, the boss asked, "May I speak with the policeman?" "No, he's busy," whispered the child. "Busy doing what?" asked the boss. "Talking to Daddy and Mommy and the fireman," came the whispered answer.

Growing concerned and even worried as he heard what sounded like a helicopter through the ear piece on the phone the boss asked, "What is that noise?" "A hello-copper," answered the whispering voice. "What is going on there?" asked the boss, now alarmed. In an awed whispering voice the child answered, "The search team just landed the hello-copper." Alarmed, concerned and more than just a little frustrated the boss asked, "What are they searching for?" Still whispering, the young voice replied along with a muffled giggle: "Me."

Woman and a Fork

There was a young woman who had been diagnosed with a terminal illness and had been given three months to live. So as she was getting her things 'in order', she contacted her Pastor and had him come to her house to discuss certain aspects of her final wishes.

She told him which songs she wanted sung at the service, what scriptures she would like read, and what outfit she wanted to be buried. Everything was in order and the Pastor was preparing to leave when the young woman suddenly remembered something very important to her.

"There's one more thing," she said excitedly. "What's that?" the Pastor replied. "This is very important," the young woman continued. "I want to be buried with a fork in my right hand." The Pastor stood looking at the young woman, not knowing quite what to say. "That surprises you, doesn't it?" she asked. "Well, to be honest, I am puzzled by the request," said the Pastor.

The young woman explained. "My grandmother once told me this story and from that time I have always tried to pass along its message to those I love and those who are in need of encouragement. In all my years of attending socials and dinners, I always remember that when the dishes of the main course were being cleared, someone would inevitably lean over and say, 'keep your fork'. It was my favorite part because I knew that something better was coming like velvety chocolate cake or deep-dish apple pie, something wonderful and with substance!"

So, I just want people to see me there in that casket with a fork in my hand and I want them to wonder "What's with the fork?" Then I want you to tell them: "Keep your fork, the best is yet to come."

The Pastor's eyes welled up with tears of joy as he hugged the young woman good-bye. He knew this would be one of the last times he would see her before her death. But he also knew that the young woman had a better grasp of heaven than he did. She had a better grasp of what heaven would be like than many people twice her age, with twice as much experience and knowledge. She KNEW that something better was coming.

At the funeral people were walking by the young woman's casket and they saw the cloak she was wearing and the fork placed in her right hand. Over and over, the Pastor heard the question, "Whats with the fork?" And over and over he smiled.

During his message, the Pastor told the people of the conversation he had with the young woman shortly before she died. He also told them about the fork and about what it symbolized to her. He told the people how he could not stop thinking about the fork and told them that they probably would not be able to stop thinking about it either. He was right. So the next time you reach down for your fork let it remind you, ever so gently, that the best is yet to come.

Friends are a very rare jewel, indeed. They make you smile and encourage you to succeed. They lend an ear, they share a word of praise, and they always want to open their hearts to us. Show your friends how much you care. Remember to always be there for them, even when you need them more. For you never know when it may be their time to "Keep your fork." Cherish the time you have and the memories you share. Being friends with someone is not an opportunity but a sweet responsibility.

And keep your fork.

Vinton & Michele Stanfield

"Where have all the children gone?"

www.ingramcontent.com/pod-product-compliance
Lightning Source LLC
LaVergne TN
LVHW051829080426
835512LV00018B/2786